TILIKUM CROSSING
BRIDGE OF THE PEOPLE

PORTLAND'S BRIDGES AND A NEW ICON

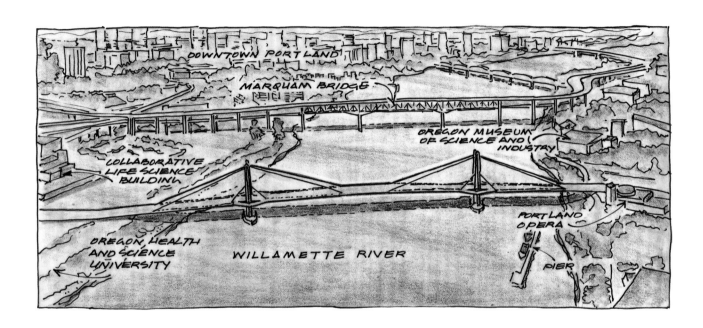

TILIKUM CROSSING
BRIDGE OF THE PEOPLE

PORTLAND'S BRIDGES AND A NEW ICON

Donald MacDonald and Ira Nadel

For Pia, Ian, Denise, and Sue
DM

For Gideon, his first book.
IN

Library of Congress Cataloging-in-Publication Data available.

ISBN: 978-0983491774

Manufactured in China.

Cover concept: Donald MacDonald
Designed by Alan Dubinsky

Overcup Press
4207 SE Woodstock Blvd. #253
Portland, Oregon 97206

www.overcupbooks.com

CONTENTS

INTRODUCTION

This is the story of the first bridge built across the Willamette River in Portland since 1973. Named Tilikum Crossing, Bridge of the People, it is unique in its automobile-free mandate. Operated by Portland's Tri-County Metropolitan Transportation District of Oregon, or TriMet, the bridge is the first cable-stayed crossing in the United States for the sole use of public transit, cyclists, and pedestrians. It is part of TriMet's MAX Orange Line light-rail service from downtown Portland to the suburbs of Milwaukie and Oak Grove (Figs. 1 & 2).

The span follows—and shares certain characteristics with—a series of other high-profile pedestrian-bridge projects (although these lack light-rail and bus traffic) in America, including the Bob Kerrey Pedestrian Bridge between Omaha, Nebraska, and Council Bluffs, Iowa, completed in 2008. But from its first day, Tilikum Crossing has been a hit locally, nationally, and internationally. Working with community groups, engineers, and owners, the San Francisco architect Donald MacDonald fashioned a cable-stayed design with relatively short towers (two towers each 180 feet tall) as the best form from an aesthetic, engineering, and construction perspective. And it is distinct, not only because it is the longest car-free span in the United States, but because it takes full advantage of its context—its angled white cables, for example, mimic the profile of majestic, snow-covered Mt. Hood visible in the distance.

Unlike other bridges over the Willamette River, functional and historical, Tilikum Crossing stands out as a structure that combines its natural setting with its purpose—and is literally a bridge of the people in that it prohibits vehicle traffic other than mass transit. People come first as it proudly stands between the Marquam Bridge (1966) and the Ross Island Bridge (1926). This book explains the process of selecting the bridge design and construction, as well as the success of the bridge, which opened on 12 September 2015 and became a new icon, immediately adopted by Portlanders as a magnificent addition to the city's distinguished history of bridges.

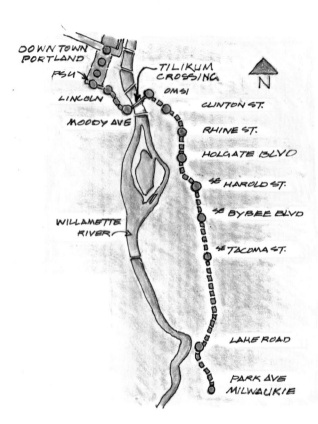

DOWNTOWN
PORTLAND
PSU
LINCOLN
MOODY AVE
TILIKUM
CROSSING
OMSI
CLINTON ST.
RHINE ST.
HOLGATE BLVD
SE HAROLD ST.
SE BYBEE BLVD
SE TACOMA ST.
WILLAMETTE
RIVER
LAKE ROAD
PARK AVE
MILWAUKIE
N

fig. 1 NEW ORANGE LINE GOING OVER
THE TILIKUM CROSSING ·
COMPLETED IN 2015

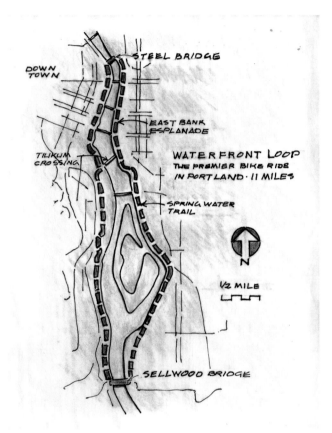

DOWN
TOWN
STEEL BRIDGE
EAST BANK
ESPLANADE
TILIKUM
CROSSING
WATERFRONT LOOP
THE PREMIER BIKE RIDE
IN PORTLAND · 11 MILES
SPRING WATER
TRAIL
N
½ MILE
SELLWOOD BRIDGE

fig. 2

1 | LIFE ON THE RIVER: NATIVE AMERICANS

Life on the river—actually the Willamette and Columbia Rivers—began thousands of years before the founding of Portland. The area was rich in natural resources, from fish to timber, essential for survival. Salmon was a prized commodity, while the wood was essential for carving canoes, building shelters, and fashioning weapons. The rivers quickly became, and remain, the transportation corridor for trade and communication.

The Chinookan peoples were once one of the most powerful and populous groups of tribes on the southern part of the Northwest Coast and still play a critical part in shaping the region through the Confederated Tribes of the Grand Ronde. Their territories originally flanked the mouth of the Columbia River and stretched up the river in a narrow band adjacent to the waterway as far as Celilo Falls, a tribal fishing area on the Columbia just east of the Cascade Mountains. One reason for their cultural prominence was their strategic position along the Columbia and proximity to Celilo Falls, the longest continuously inhabited site in the Americas, used as a fishing site and trading hub for 15,000 years by numerous indigenous peoples. Construction of The Dalles Dam in 1957, however, submerged the falls and nearby settlements.

Importantly, the Chinookan peoples were not nomadic but, rather, occupied and maintained traditional tribal geographic areas. Social stratification marked their society, which contained a number of distinct social groups of greater or lesser status. Upper castes included shamans, warriors, and successful traders, a minority of the community population compared to common members of the tribal group. Members of the superior castes practiced social isolation, limiting contact with commoners and even forbidding play between the children of the different social groups.

As late as the early 19th century, the Chinookan-speaking peoples resided along the lower and middle Columbia River in present-day Oregon and Washington. The Lewis and Clark Expedition encountered the Chinook tribes on the lower Columbia in October–November 1805. According to Thomas Jefferson, one of Lewis and Clark's goals was to find "the most direct and practicable water communication across this continent, for the purposes of commerce." Jefferson also placed special importance on declaring U.S. sovereignty over the land occupied by the different tribes of Native Americans along the Missouri River, while getting an accurate sense of the resources in the recently completed Louisiana Purchase.

Ironically, although the Chinookan peoples have lived on the lower Columbia River for millennia, the lower Chinooks from the mouth of the Columbia River remain unrecognized by the U.S. government. The Chinookan people from the area of the Tilikum Crossing bridge are the Clackamas and signed treaties with the U.S. government. The lower Chinook tribal territory followed the movement of the Columbia River, beginning at the Pacific Ocean and working inland up the Columbia to current day Cascade Locks and on the Willamette River from its mouth to just upstream of Willamette Falls (Fig. 3).

Preceding Portland as a settler trade center was Oregon City because of its location near Willamette Falls. This area became the pivot of early settler trading activities, mostly logging and fishing, before moving further downriver to what would become Portland. The area around Willamette Falls as well as Celilo Falls were centers of trade for native people for thousands of years before settlers used these areas for many of the same purposes. Importantly, the Chinookan peoples clustered in distinct Plankhouses along the lower Willamette and Columbia Rivers (Fig. 4).

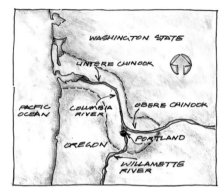

TRADITIONAL CHINOOK TRIBAL TERRITORY IN THE LOWER COLUMBIA RIVER BASIN

fig. 3

TYPICAL CHINOOK INDIAN HOUSING CLUSTER ON THE WILLAMETTE RIVER · PART OF THE COLUMBIA RIVER BASIN

fig. 4

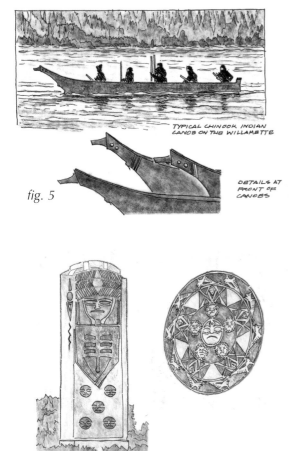

TYPICAL CHINOOK INDIAN
CANOE ON THE WILLAMETTE

DETAILS AT
FRONT OF
CANOES

fig. 5

fig. 6

Plankhouses were typical of Native American housing along the Pacific Ocean and the northwest coast. They were constructed of vertical cedar wall panels visible in the roofing, the panels joined by split planks. The roofs also had a hole to let smoke out from their fires, while communal sleeping was common. Their long canoes, dug out of cedar and able to carry five to a few dozen occupants, became their main source of transportation, creating a sophisticated travel system able to weather both the rivers and the sea (Fig. 5).

The Chinookan peoples continue to contribute to the culture and economy of the Northwest. Three new works of art by Chinookan artist Greg A. Robinson created in the Columbia River Art tradition are placed at the east and west ends of the Tilikum Crossing. Entitled "We Have Always Lived Here," the works were donated by the Confederated Tribes of Grande Ronde to commemorate the Chinook peoples of the lower Columbia. The first is the five-foot-diameter bronze medallion on the eastern side retaining wall; the second and third are six-foot-tall basalt column carvings, or power poles, that stand near the bike/pedestrian paths of the east side of the bridge and in the middle of the trackway on the west side (Fig. 6).

The history of Portland is the history of its bridges. Founded in 1845 with the flip of a coin—the two founders competed for the name, the one from Massachusetts wanting Boston, the one from Maine preferring Portland—the city has always been defined by its location. As a major shipping port for the Pacific Northwest's lumber, wheat, and other resources, it quickly grew in population and size. The confluence of the Columbia and Willamette Rivers made it possible for seagoing vessels to reach the port. A horse-powered ferry across the Willamette River began in 1848, replaced in 1853 by a steam-driven ferry. By the 1860s, the need for a bridge to increase the movement of goods and people became acute.

Resistance by ferry and navigation interests delayed progress, but a Willamette Bridge Company was formed in 1886, and gradually permission and then construction of the Morrison Street Bridge got underway. This was a timber bridge 1,650 feet long with a wrought-iron swing span. It opened on 2 March 1887. The tolls were 5 cents for pedestrians, 20 cents for two horses and driver, with the driver's family riding for free.

A year later, the double-deck Steel Bridge opened, the first steel bridge on the West Coast and built by a subsidiary of the Union Pacific Railroad. The use of steel as opposed to wrought iron gave it a special distinction. A swing span bridge, the lower deck was for rail traffic and the upper for vehicles. Postcards of the bridge began to circulate shortly after its opening. Geographically at this point, the Willamette River makes a 45-degree bend between the Steel and what would be the Burnside Bridge (Fig. 7).

Bridge construction suddenly took off. Two years later construction started on the Madison Street Bridge, completed in June 1891. This was a timber bridge with a swing span. It was built as a private venture, gaining revenue from its tolls. That same year the state legislature established a committee to investigate buying, building, or leasing one or more suitable bridges across the Willamette and began by purchasing the Madison Street Bridge for $145,000 in November 1891. They immediately, in a sign of largesse, removed the tolls. They then bid to purchase the Morrison Bridge but were rejected.

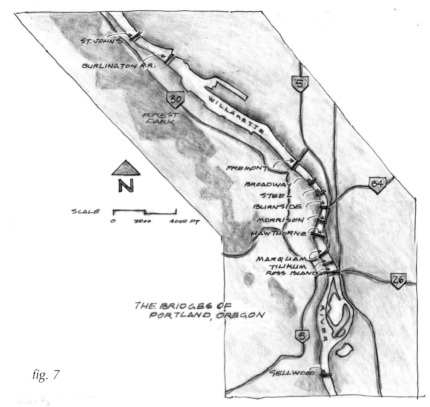

fig. 7

A proposal for two new bridges at this time was rejected by the Army Corps of Engineers, who had control over the access to and over the river. Determined to succeed, the state committee appealed directly to the Secretary of War in Washington and convinced him of its need. A contract to build the Burnside Street Bridge was granted in 1892, and two years later in 1894 the new, wrought-iron-and-steel bridge of 1,621 feet with a swing span was opened—without tolls. But with increased river traffic, the bridge opened an average of 27 times a day, disrupting vehicles and pedestrians.

The swing span on these early bridges was necessary because ships became taller as well as larger. But of course, swing spans delayed the crossing of traffic and became increasingly a nuisance. Clearance for navigation became a constant problem, and as late as 1989, the Willamette River Railroad bridge owner (the Burlington Northern Railroad) removed the swing span and center pier, installing a single vertical lift span and towers. At its construction, which began in August 1906, the swing span was the largest in the world. Soon postcards recorded the open span, one showing it perpendicular to the roadway.

The length of the swing span was 524 feet, 2 inches with a 4.6-million-pound weight. The drum beneath it, allowing it to swing, was 42 feet in diameter. The combination of the swing span and its adjacent fixed spans on either side created a wonderful mix of movable and fixed elements. The designer was Ralph Modjeski. The 1989 shift was made in a remarkable 72-hour period and eliminated numerous collisions by ships with the bridge, especially its center pier. The new vertical lift drawbridge—the two towers at either side lifted up the main span railway—increased river traffic and safety.

Bridges do not last forever, and the timber-built Madison Street Bridge deteriorated rapidly. In 1900 it was rebuilt with new timber members and with a reinforced swing span. The Morrison Bridge was also falling into disrepair. Bids for a new wrought-iron-and-steel replacement were received in 1904, but politics played a hand, resulting in the need for reform.

By this time, responsibility for bridge building was transferred from the city of Portland to Multnomah County, which in the 1920s began an ambitious rebuilding program. Starting with a replacement of the Burnside Bridge and construction of the Ross Island Bridge and the Sellwood Bridge in the 1920s, Portlanders understood the importance of their bridges. In that decade voters approved a $4.5 million bond issue to build two fixed-span bridges, the Ross Island and Sellwood

Bridges, and to replace the slow-opening swing-span Burnside Bridge, which opened in 1894. During this period, however, graft also became noticeable, and taxpayers learned that the Burnside Bridge construction contract was let for half a million dollars more than the lowest bid. Criminal indictments followed. New county commissioners, replacing three who were recalled, hired Pacific Bridge Co. to build the bridge and retained Gustav Lindenthal to take over the design and construction.

Suddenly, nationally known designers began to compete for the work. When replacements were needed for the Steel Bridge and Madison Bridge (a second Steel Bridge and the new Hawthorne Bridge), the consulting engineers came from Kansas City, Missouri, and Chicago. The well-respected Ralph Modjeski of Chicago designed the Hawthorne Street Bridge, as well as three large swing-type drawbridges for the Northern Pacific Railway on the Columbia River and so-called Oregon Slough between Portland and nearby Vancouver, Washington. These were built in 1908. An interstate bridge between Portland and Vancouver over the Columbia River was built between 1915 and 1917.

Construction of the St. Johns Bridge, designed by Robinson and Steinman of New York, began just before the Wall Street Crash of 1929. Construction was completed, however, in 1931, providing Portland with its only suspension bridge and the largest suspension bridge west of the Mississippi. The main span was 1,207 feet.

Following World War II, the next major project began in 1958, a replacement of the Morrison Bridge with a double-leaf bascule–type drawbridge similar to the Burnside Bridge. Also in 1958, a twin bridge was added to the Interstate Bridge, altering (actually raising it by replacing two 275-foot trusses with one 550-foot truss) the original bridge to allow more marine traffic to pass without needing to open the bridge.

A controversy emerged with the next bridge, however: the Marquam Bridge, a double-deck, steel-cantilevered truss bridge between the Ross Island and Hawthorne Bridges. Designed by the Oregon State Highway Department, it was to close the link in Interstate 5 and make the freeway continuous from the California border to the Columbia River. But its utilitarian form prompted a protest from the Portland arts community. In response, the next bridge for Interstate 405 to cross the Willamette River north of the Broadway Bridge was more aesthetically pleasing, designed with the assistance of the Parsons Brinckerhoff firm of New York.

This new Fremont Bridge opened in 1973. It is a tied arch, steel design with a lengthy 1,255-foot main span. Finally, the Jackson Memorial Bridge opened in 1982, which completed the eastside bypass of Interstate 205. It is a post-tensioned concrete box girder structure. Importantly, all the bridges in this brief narrative of the bridges of Portland were designed for vehicle traffic, notably cars, trucks, and rail. One among many distinguishing features of Tilikum Crossing is that it is not. "No cars or trucks allowed" might be the motto for Portland's newest bridge.

In less than a decade after the first Morrison Bridge opened in 1887, three more bridges were constructed, and these bridges encouraged a population boom: in 1880 there were 17,600 residents. By 1900 the number grew to 90,000. Almost a hundred years later in 1988, eight bridges crossed a three-mile section of the Willamette River, with now fifteen crossings the combined total of bridges across the Willamette and Columbia Rivers within Portland itself.

Unique, perhaps, to the range of bridges is their diversity: drawbridges, suspension bridges, tied arch, and other forms exist, revealing a history of bridge construction as much as the city. Several of the bridges set records when they were built. One of them is the world's only double-deck, vertical lift bridge capable of raising the lower deck independently of the upper. Another is a rare example of a Rall bascule–type drawbridge. Bascule is French for "seesaw." A bascule bridge allows the roadway to tilt upward, allowing river traffic to pass; it uses counterweights to balance the weight of the lift span. There are two types: either single leaf with one hinge or double with two. The Broadway, Burnside, and Morrison bridges are the three bascule bridges over the Willamette, all double leaf.

This tradition of bridges in Portland is the context for the city's newest bridge, Tilikum Crossing, opening to the public in September 2015. Just north of the new bridge stands the older Marquam Bridge, which opened in 1966 and is today one of Oregon's most heavily trafficked bridges, carrying 135,000 cars across the river per day. But with two decks and a squat frame, the older bridge at best looks functional and makes Tilikum seem delicate and almost floating in the air.

Below is a chronological listing of Portland's major bridges with comments on their individual engineering and design.

BRIDGES: A CHRONOLOGY

Note: River mile 0 is between Sauvie Island and Kelley Point at the confluence of the Willamette and Columbia Rivers. Geographically and moving south (upstream), the bridges are the St. Johns, Fremont, Broadway, Steel, Burnside, Morrison, Hawthorne, Marquam, Tilikum Crossing, Ross Island, and farther to the south, the Sellwood.

The Morrison Bridge, 1887. River mile 12.8. Swing span for the 1887 and 1905 bridges; steel truss with one double-leaf bascule movable main span for the 1958 bridge. Color: aluminum gray (1958). The 1887 original bridge was the first bridge across the lower Willamette River, replaced in 1905 and outfitted to carry streetcars. A sign on the original bridge at mid-span read "Walk your horses on the Draw." A new Morrison Bridge was built in 1958, alongside the 1905 bridge, which was soon dismantled.

The name originated with the street it serves, named itself after John L. Morrison (1819–99), who built the first house on what is a main thoroughfare extending east and west across the Willamette. He was a carpenter who emigrated from Scotland in 1831 and voted with 50 others to establish the provisional government of Oregon (Fig. 8).

SHOWN IN AN OPEN POSITION

MORRISON BRIDGE IS A BASCULE TYPE BRIDGE · COMPLETED IN 1958

fig. 8

Steel Bridge, 1888 (lower rail deck) 1889 (upper vehicle deck) + replacement in 1912 with its double-lift structure. River mile 12.1. Color: gun-metal black (1912). Originally a swing span truss bridge, it was partly made out of steel (hence its name) and timber, which would occasionally catch fire, often caused by burning material from the exhaust of a crossing locomotive. The main span is 211 feet made out of steel. It was the first railroad bridge across the Willamette River at Portland. The 1912 replacement was by Waddell & Harrington, Kansas City, Missouri. The Steel Bridge remains the only double-deck, telescoping vertical lift bridge in the world. The lower deck was built for trains and may be lifted independently; the upper deck was built for street railways, pedestrians, and other vehicles. Both decks may be lifted together. Raising only the lower deck permits small river craft to pass. In 1986, Metropolitan Area Express (MAX) light rail was added. In 2001, River Walk opened across the bottom deck of the bridge (Fig. 9).

Madison Bridge, 1891. Swing span and truss built of timber at the site of the current Hawthorne Bridge. Color: wood. Deterioration meant a rebuild of the bridge in 1899 with a strengthened swing span (316 feet), reinforced by building a tower over the center pier and connecting iron or steel rods from the tower to the ends of the swing span. All new timber trusses for the six 190-foot fixed spans east of the swing span also occurred. The worst bridge disaster in Portland occurred in 1893 on the Madison Bridge when a motorman disregarded a red signal during heavy fog, causing his trolley car to plunge into the Willamette River; seven people drowned. The Hawthorne Bridge replaced the Madison.

Burnside Bridge, 1894, 1926. River mile 12.4. Color: yellow ochre with towers of red, beige, and green. Originally a swing-span bridge, it was renovated in 1926. The trusses for the new bridge were originally designed by Hedrick & Kremers, Portland, but after Robert Kremers was arrested for bribery and collusion, Gustav Lindenthal took over. Joseph Strauss of Chicago was responsible for the bascule, the form that allows the roadway to split and tilt upward on either side to allow ships to pass through. It uses counterweights

STEEL BRIDGE · THROUGH TRUSS · DOUBLE DECK VERTICAL
LIFT BRIDGE IN AN OPEN POSITION   CONSTUCTED IN 1912

fig. 9

BURNSIDE BRIDGE IS A BASCULE TYPE BRIDGE
COMPLETED IN 1926
PLACED ON THE NATIONAL REGISTER OF HISTORIC PLACES IN 2012

fig. 10

(concrete weights are located one each inside Burnside's two river piers) to balance the weight of the lift span. The Burnside Bridge is a double-leaf bascule, meaning both sides of the roadway swing upward. Technically, the bridge has three steel deck truss spans with one double-leaf bascule movable main span with two fixed side spans. Named after Dan Wyman Burnside (1825–1887), Portland businessman (Fig. 10).

Burlington Northern Railroad Bridge, 1908. River mile 6.9. Built by the Spokane, Portland, and Seattle Railway. The Burlington Northern Railroad Bridge is a through truss railway bridge, owned and operated by Burlington Northern Santa Fe Railway. It was originally a swing-span bridge completed in 1908. A committee of Port of Portland officials originally recommended a bascule-type bridge. However, the swing span was ultimately accepted. Eighty-one years later it was renovated and transformed into a vertical lift bridge. It is a 1763-foot-long structure with a 516-foot-long vertical lift. The lift provides clearance of 200 feet at low water, making it one of the highest and longest of this type of bridge in the world. The new lift weighs 7,900,000 pounds.

The bridge carries two railroad tracks, which are used by BNSF, Union Pacific Railroad, and Amtrak. Signals from both sides prevent trains from entering when the lift span is up. Trains must also radio the bridge tender and gain permission to cross. It is the only bridge in the Portland area not open to the public and rail only. The Burlington Northern Railroad Bridge was the first bridge of any kind to be built across the lower Columbia River, preceding the first road bridge, the nearby Interstate Bridge, by a little more than eight years. The lift span of the bridge is made of weathering steel, which rusts naturally and makes the lift a reddish brown color. The rest of the bridge is painted silver (Fig. 11).

Hawthorne Street Bridge, 1910. River mile 13.1. Vertical lift. Truss designed by Waddell & Harrington, Kansas City, Missouri. Color: green with red trim. This is the oldest vertical lift bridge in North America, followed by the Steel Bridge, and stands only 49 feet above the river. The design engineer John A.L. Waddell independently invented and introduced the high-clearance vertical lift bridge in Chicago, and his firm designed the

COUNTER WEIGHT

BURLINGTON RAILROAD BRIDGE · THROUGH TRUSS
VERTICAL LIFT BRIDGE · COMPLETED 1908 MAIN SPAN
REPLACED 1989 · SHOWN IN A CLOSED POSITION

fig. 11

Hawthorne Bridge, which opened three years before Portland got its first traffic light. The original bridge had a wooden deck, replaced by steel in 1945, which lasted until 1998. The lift span rises on average 120 times a month. The Hawthorne Bridge replaced the Madison Bridge No. 2 (1900), which replaced Madison Bridge No. 1 (1891) after a fire. Named after Dr. J.C. Hawthorne (1819–81) who helped found the Oregon Hospital for the Insane. He was an early advocate of the Morrison Bridge in 1887 (Fig. 12).

Broadway Bridge, 1913. River mile 11.7. Double-leaf bascule bridge with trusses. Color: originally red with a tinge of International Orange, the color to be used on the Golden Gate Bridge in San Francisco. Designed by the world-renowned Ralph Modjeski of Chicago, it was the longest double-leaf bascule drawbridge in the world when it opened. Portland had outgrown its ferry system and needed lighter-weight bridges, as well as a bridge downriver from the Steel Bridge. The Broadway Bridge also marked an ownership change from the city of Portland to Multnomah County. The name of the bridge derives from the main connecting street, Broadway. Composed of one movable and five fixed spans, it is an example of a Rall-type bascule span, named after the inventor (Theodor Rall) of its complicated opening method that permits each lift span of 148.5 feet in length to rise on its hinged Rall wheels. The counterweighted leaves slide backward and upward on eight-foot-diameter wheels. Each leaf, with its above-deck counterweight, weighs 2,000 tons. Electric rail cars were the main form of city transportation when it opened (Fig. 13).

Sellwood Bridge, 1925. River mile 16.5. Fixed span, truss. Color: green. Gustav Lindenthal designed the truss spans for what was Portland's first fixed-span bridge. Engineering by this time could build bridges high enough to accommodate river traffic and no longer needed to disrupt vehicle traffic with lift bridges. Between 1887 and 1925, all major Portland bridges across the Willamette moved. The Sellwood Bridge replaced the Spokane Street Ferry but from the first day was considered too narrow for vehicles, especially westbound heading downtown. It was only two lanes with no shoulders or center median and only one sidewalk plus no trolley tracks.

COUNTER WEIGHT

HAWTHORNE BRIDGE · TRUSS BRIDGE VERTICAL LIFT SHOWN
CLOSED · BUILT IN 1910 · ON THE NATIONAL REGISTER OF
HISTORIC PLACES IN 2012

fig. 12

BROADWAY BRIDGE · RALL·TYPE BASCULE BRIDGE
BUILT IN 1913 · WORLD'S LONGEST DOUBLE·LEAF BASCULE
PLACED ON THE NATIONAL REGISTER OF HISTORIC PLACES IN 2012

fig. 13

Because of its aging, there was a reduction of maximum bridge loads to ten tons in 2004, forcing most trucks and buses to use an alternate crossing. The bridge did not age well, with cracks in the concrete and an inability to resist earthquake forces resulting in what engineers term "low sufficiency." The bridge was unusual for its asymmetrical vertical curve providing a transition from the flat land at its east end to the steeply sloping west end. A bridge kick-back scandal necessitated the replacement of the Portland firm of Hedrick & Kremers with Gustav Lindenthal. The scandal also involved the Ross Island and Burnside Bridges (Fig. 14).

In 2016, the Sellwood Bridge was replaced by a new deck arch bridge. The new Sellwood Bridge was designed by T.Y. Lin and built by Slayden/Sundt.

The bridge is named after the community of

SELLWOOD REPLACEMENT BRIDGE·MULTNOMAH COUNTY·COMPLETED IN 2016 'STEEL ARCH TYPE BRIDGE'

fig. 14

Sellwood, itself named for an earlier settler from South Carolina, Reverend James R.W. Sellwood.

Ross Island Bridge, 1926. River mile 14. Fixed span, cantilevered deck truss bridge, designed by Gustav Lindenthal of New York, composed of five steel spans with an arch-shaped main span. Color: brilliant, rich blue, also known as "phthalo" blue, a synthetic blue pigment. The first downtown bridge to be built without streetcar tracks, reflecting the increase in automobile use in Portland. Within a few months of its opening, Charles Lindbergh flew the Spirit of St. Louis to Portland to celebrate his historic solo flight to France. The Ross Island Bridge began the Mount Hood Highway System. It also allowed pedestrians on both sides, but in 1958 the south side sidewalk was removed to widen the bridge for cars and trucks. It is the heaviest traveled nonfreeway bridge in Portland and is the only bridge on the river to carry water pipes on its superstructure. The name derives from the three-island group located just south of the span. Sherry Ross was a pioneer settler on the largest island (Fig. 15).

St. Johns Bridge, 1931. River mile 5.8. Fixed span, suspension bridge. Color: verdant green. This bridge is the only major suspension bridge in the Willamette Valley, forming a symbolic gateway to

ROSS ISLAND BRIDGE COMPLETED 1926.
CANTILEVER DECK TRUSS BRIDGE

fig. 15

MAIN SPAN 1207'
TOWER HEIGHT 400'
NAVIGATIONAL
CLEARANCE 205'

MAIN CABLE
SUSPENDERS

WILLAMETTE RIVER

ST. JOHN'S BRIDGE · PORTLAND · AT THE TIME OF CONSTUCTION
(1931) IT WAS LONGEST SUSPENSION IN THE WEST

fig. 16

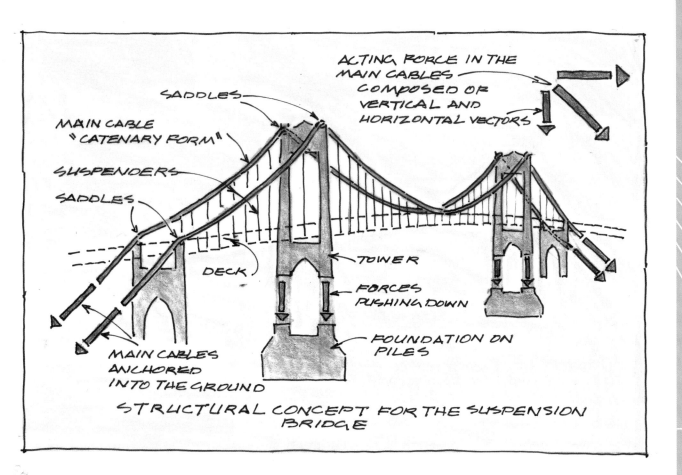

ACTING FORCE IN THE MAIN CABLES COMPOSED OF VERTICAL AND HORIZONTAL VECTORS

SADDLES

MAIN CABLE "CATENARY FORM"

SUSPENDERS

SADDLES

DECK

TOWER

FORCES PUSHING DOWN

FOUNDATION ON PILES

MAIN CABLES ANCHORED INTO THE GROUND

STRUCTURAL CONCEPT FOR THE SUSPENSION BRIDGE

fig. 17

Portland. When it opened in 1931, it had the longest span of any suspension bridge west of the Ambassador Bridge in Detroit. Seven miles from downtown Portland, it connects the North Portland communities of St. Johns on the east end with Linnton on the west. The design engineers were David B. Steinman and Holton Robinson of New York. The two-tower suspension bridge has a tower height to the water of 400 feet. The main span length is 1,207 feet.

Some 26,000 Portlanders signed a petition in 1924 for construction of the bridge, beginning a five-year battle with opponents who thought that North Portland was too sparsely populated to justify such an expensive structure. This occurred during Portland's so-called "bridge fever" years, when the Oregon City (1922), Sellwood (1925), Burnside (1926), and Ross Island (1926) Bridges were opened. But many objected to the $4.25 million bond issue necessary to build the bridge and the increase in taxes. Nonetheless, voters approved the bridge in November 1928, and construction began one month before the so-called Black Thursday

of 24 October 1929, when the stock market crashed (Figs. 16 & 17).

Marquam Bridge, 1966. River mile: 13.5. Three-span double-deck cantilever truss bridge with a suspended section in the main span just north of Tilikum Crossing. Color: concrete gray. Portland's first Willamette freeway bridge. South of downtown, it completed the first half of the city's inner freeway loop and completed the last gap in Interstate 5 from Canada south to Mexico. It is utilitarian rather than beautiful, causing the Portland Art Commission to make a formal protest to the governor over its lack of design. Engineers supported its simplicity and economy of design. Nonetheless, it is Portland's busiest bridge, with over 140,000 cars crossing it per day. Named after the early settler and member of the state legislature Philip A. Marquam (1828–1912) (Fig. 18).

Fremont Bridge, 1973. River mile 11.1. Designed by Parsons, Brinckerhoff, Quade, and Douglas, New York. Color: light green. Located five miles upstream from the St. Johns Bridge and noticeable by its center arch, 381 feet above the water and 902 feet long, the

MARQUAM BRIDGE · DOUBLE-DECK STEEL-TRUSS
CANTILEVER BRIDGE COMPLETED 1966

fig. 18

MAIN SPAN OF BRIDGE : 1255'
CLEARANCE UNDER THE
BRIDGE : 175'

SUSPENDERS

FREMONT BRIDGE · PORTLAND · AT THE TIME OF
CONSTRUCTION (1973) IT WAS THE SECOND LONGEST
TIED-ARCH BRIDGE IN THE WORLD

fig. 19

Labels within image: MAIN SPAN OF BRIDGE = 1400', SUSPENDERS, YANGTZE RIVER

CAIYUANBA BRIDGE ACROSS THE YANGTZE RIVER.
YUZHONG. CHINA. LONGEST TIED-ARCH BRIDGE AT
THE TIME OF CONSTRUCTION (1978) IN THE WORLD

fig. 20

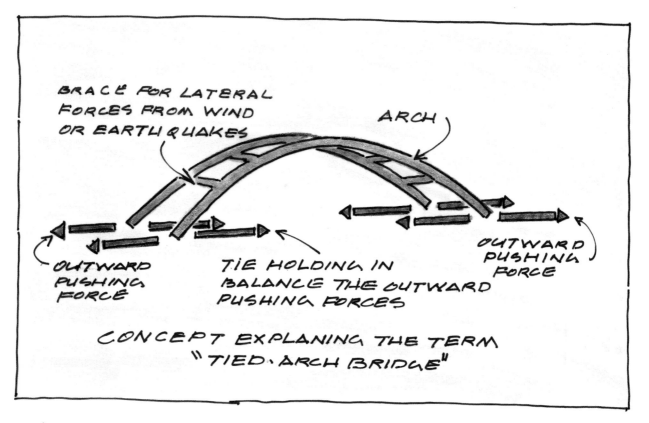

fig. 21

40

Fremont Bridge also has the longest bridge structure in the Oregon highway system at 1,255 feet for the main span designed without bridge supports in the central channel. It incorporates an arch span and box girder design and was the longest arch bridge of its type in the world until the new Caiyuanba Bridge across the Yangtze River in Chongqing, China, opened in 2004. It is now the second-longest tied-arch bridge in the world. The lift for the center span was a 50-hour process using 32 hydraulic jacks, eight at each corner. The bridge provides 175 feet of clearance for tall ships.

The roadway, interestingly, passes though the arch, the upper deck carrying westbound traffic, the lower suspended from the upper deck carrying eastbound traffic. A more aesthetically successful bridge than the Marquam, it cost six times as much. The name originated with Fremont Street, which at one time was to be eastside approached. John Charles Frémont (1813–90) was the namesake of the street, an explorer and army officer (Figs. 19–21).

Tilikum Crossing, Bridge of the People, 2015. Between river mile 14 and 13.5. Color: white. It was designed by Donald MacDonald of San Francisco working for TriMet and partnered with HNTB for the first 30% completion of the structural design. At the 30% stage, the prescribed design went to bid, and the best-priced contract was won by T.Y. Lin engineers with Kiewit construction. Light rail and bus transit ways are separated from pedestrian and bicycle lanes to form the longest car-free transit bridge in the United States. It is a cable-stayed bridge using a fan system, the cables fanning out from the top of two 180-foot towers. The bridge links education, research, and job centers, such as Oregon Health Sciences University in the South Waterfront of Portland with the Eastside location of Oregon Museum of Science and Industry, Portland Opera, and recreational facilities.

CHAPTER

3 | CHOICES

Portland enjoys an international reputation as the "City of Bridges." Adding a new crossing to the existing bridges has important implications for the city's skyline and overall bridge pattern. For urban context, each bridge must be examined as fitting into this fabric. For Tilikum Crossing, this meant compatibility with the adjacent Ross Island and Marquam Bridges and the proposed development on either bank of the river where the bridge meets the shoreline.

Before the selection of the cable-stayed form of Tilikum Crossing, a series of other proposals were presented, each with special features that capitalized on the location. Of initial importance, however, was the proximity of adjacent bridges and the integration of a new, scaled bridge structure that would not tower over the other bridges along the river. The bridge's location near earthquake fault lines was also a major concern in the design of its overall structure and choice of bridge form.

Portland has three major fault lines in the area: the Oatfield Fault to the west of Portland proper, the Portland Hills Fault, which runs through the center of the city, and the East Bank Fault across the Willamette almost parallel to Interstate 5. These earthquake zones would naturally impact on the design, materials, and structural form of any potential crossing. Hazard maps prepared by the city of Portland clearly outlined the fault lines, the Portland Hills Fault running almost directly under the western foundation of the Tilikum Crossing bridge.

Nonetheless, experts indicated that the new bridge, plus the Marquam (I-5) and the new Sellwood Bridge, should survive, since they were built to new, exacting earthquake standards. All bridges with counterweights would collapse, however. A tsunami and liquefaction remain constant worries (Fig. 22).

Bedrock or glacial till, the main land components also affect the stability of land in a major earthquake, and both elements are stable. Unlike Seattle, Portland does not have a massive basin underneath to amplify the motions and is a little farther from the Cascadia fault. But the real issue is the possibility of a full-margin rupture of the Cascadia subduction zone, which runs some 700 miles off the Pacific coast from California to Vancouver Island, Canada.

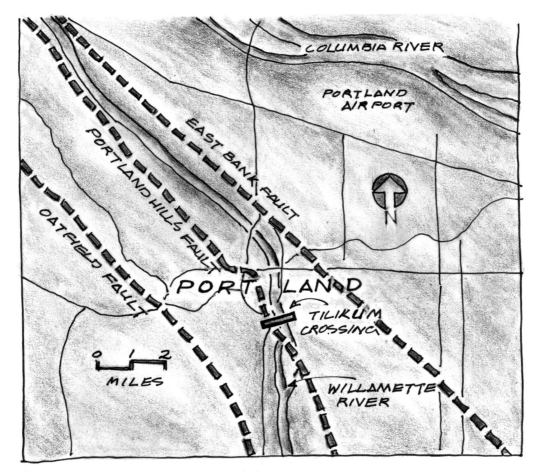

MAP SHOWING MAJOR FAULT LINES IN THE PORTLAND AREA

fig. 22

The study of seismic effects in national building and bridge codes didn't improve in earnest until the late 1980s. Buildings and bridges, like many of those in Portland, built to codes before this time didn't benefit from the improved knowledge gained from the past three decades of seismic observations, understanding, and code improvements. As such, serious damage is expected to follow such an event. The old bridges downtown would also not survive serious tremors. Virtually all the city's fuel supplies (gasoline, jet fuel, oil), stored in tank farms on an island in the river where the soil would liquefy, pose another hazard. In Seattle, some of the major bridges have been upgraded, including I-5 and 99 over the ship canal, so they would not be likely to topple. But in much of the region, the ground would likely turn to soup from liquefaction. Portland also has numerous brick buildings that would crumble. Neighborhoods would be cut off and on their own because first responders would be literally swamped.

Bridge proposals for Tilikum Crossing reflected an awareness of the fault zones and potential dangers to a new structure. Proposals ranged from a through-arch bridge similar to the Fremont Bridge and a tied-arch bridge to a hybrid bridge that mixed a suspension and cable-stayed system. One of the more experimental proposals, the third, was an extradosed bridge, a post tension bridge and a cross between a girder bridge and cable-stayed bridge. In an extradosed bridge, the deck is directly supported by resting on part of the tower, so that close to the tower the deck can act as a continuous beam. The cables from a lower tower intersect with the deck only farther out, and at a lower angle, so that their tension acts more to compress the bridge deck horizontally than to support it vertically. Thus, the cable stays act as pre-stressing cables for a concrete deck. The term extradosed comes from the French extradossée, derived from extrados, the exterior curve of an arch. Such bridges are expensive and inefficient in their use of materials (Fig. 23).

Miguel Rosales of Rosales + Partners, Boston, was selected to do a preliminary study of bridge types as part of the first phase. These choices echoed, if not imitated, existing Portland bridge structures. They were not

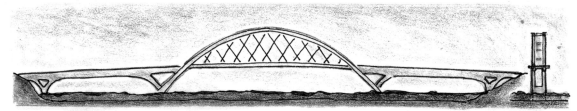

THROUGH ARCH BRIDGE · SIMILAR TO THE FREMONT   SECTION
TIED · ARCH BRIDGE

HYBRID BRIDGE · SUSPENSION AND CABLE STAYED   SECTION
SYSTEMS IN PLACE · SIMILAR TO THE BROOKLYN
BRIDGE IN NEW YORK BUILT AND COMPLETED IN 1883

EXTRADOSED BRIDGE   SECTION
TOWER HEIGHTS · NOT AN APPROPRIATE PROPORTION 1/2 ABOVE
AND 1/2 BELOW DECK

fig. 23

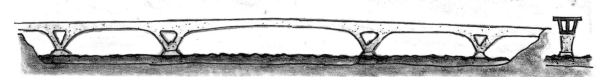

CONCRETE SEGMENTAL BOX BRIDGE   SECTION

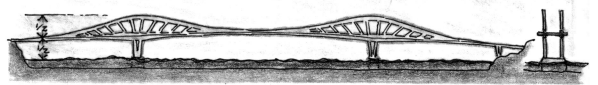

WAVE FRAME GIRDER BRIDGE
WAVE HEIGHTS · NOT AN APPROPRIATE PROPORTION 1/2
ABOVE AND 1/2 BELOW DECK   SECTION

SAIL BLADE GIRDER BRIDGE
TOWER HEIGHTS · NOT AN APPROPRIATE PROPORTION 1/2
ABOVE AND 1/2 BELOW DECK   SECTION

fig. 24

47

accepted. Additional proposals by Rosales did not make it to the final selection: a concrete segmental box bridge with the cables inside, and a wave-frame girder bridge, expensive and visually unpleasant partly because it impeded views from the deck's surface because of its form.

A third option was a sail-blade girder bridge, with an inadequate proportion following a half-above-deck and half-below-deck principle. Preferable proportions use the rule of thirds with the towers and cables one-third above the roadway, which is two-thirds above the water line. This divides the eye and is more intriguing from a design perspective (Fig. 24).

TriMet initiated a second design phase after these preliminary studies. They turned to MacDonald Architects, San Francisco, for the final, prescribed design/build contract. The second phase produced an experienced West Coast designer familiar with the conditions, geography, and environment of the region.

Other bridge types were also recommended but rejected because they did not display the uniqueness required for a bridge of the 21st century. A bridge should be symbolic while reflecting the progressive nature of this century (Fig. 25).

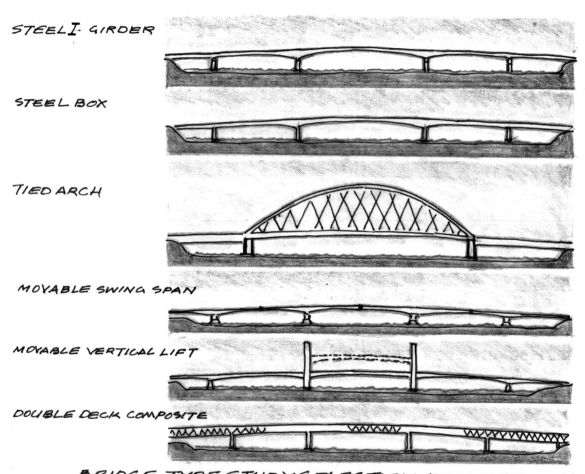

STEEL I-GIRDER

STEEL BOX

TIED ARCH

MOVABLE SWING SPAN

MOVABLE VERTICAL LIFT

DOUBLE DECK COMPOSITE

BRIDGE TYPE STUDY SELECTION PROCESS

fig. 25

The public process of selecting the final design for Tilikum Crossing was as intriguing as the aesthetic decisions and engineering challenges. A series of public consultations sponsored by TriMet, following lengthy work by a selection committee and a volunteer public advisory committee, meant hours of involvement in neighborhoods, city council meetings, engineering consultations, and consultations with environmentalists, bicycle enthusiasts, and designers. Yet the initial goals were straightforward: a structure compatible with an expanded current light-rail system, to remain within a set budget and be completed within 44 months. Additionally, the bridge had to embody the Portland aesthetic of outdoor living and appreciation of the arts, fresh foods, great coffee, and bicycling, as well as be functional and affordable.

The project also had to be environmentally responsible and the result of a so-called "open decision-making process." Not only would the public be involved, but TriMet hoped to offer contracts to small businesses and businesses operated by minorities to ensure an inclusive project. The use of advanced, three-dimensional visual depictions illustrating designs and impact assessment would assist both the committee's and the public's decision-making process.

For this project, public involvement meant contributing to the conception, final design, and even construction of the bridge. First, a committee representing design, transportation, business, and community leaders began the selection process, beginning with a presentation from technical staff representing the project partners and consultants. They evaluated selection criteria and prepared reports and recommendations. Before public consultation, however, the technical group presented to the selection committee the range of possible bridge types. A month later, the committee revised bridge study goals as they moved from the "universe" of bridges to a select number of choices. Semyon Treyger/ HNTB, a distinguished structural engineer, played a crucial part in re-formulating the world of possible bridge types. He would also collaborate with Donald MacDonald in the development of the final scheme used in the RFP (request for proposal) and final engineering.

The creative dynamic between the structural engineer and architect established an important design/build ethic that filtered throughout the entire project, as Robert Hastings, Agency Architect of TriMet, and a critical facilitator for the entire process from the first day, confirmed. The application of a "project first" approach was used to resolve conflicts within the team, ensuring that Kiewit and T.Y. Lin would not deviate from the nature and details articulated by MacDonald and Treyger. The unique approach immeasurably contributed to meeting budget, schedule, and design goals.

But certain issues remained paramount, notably river navigation in relation to bridge alignment and the impact of alignment on viable bridge types, plus compatibility with the existing bridges. The proposed bridge would also interface with two riverbank greenways, navigational users of the river, and riverside wildlife habitats (Figs. 26–30). The recommended alignment was approved by the appropriate committees in summer 2008.

Initially, there were twenty-two bridge types, including movable, cable-supported, and arch (see Chapter 3). The HNTB Corporation, a civil engineering consulting and construction management firm founded in 1914 with headquarters in Kansas City, Missouri, organized and executed the overall selection process with TriMet and the Willamette River Bridge Advisory Committee. HNTB had experience designing bridges, roadways, rail, and transit systems across the United States and around the world.

The Advisory Committee began to meet regularly with Trimet to evaluate the types of bridges that would meet the requirements of budget and length (1,720 feet). Other requirements included being aesthetically balanced with the city, create a minimal effect on the environment and river, and be a landmark and signature image for Portland.

More technically, experts noted that a minimum deck span of 600 feet between the two center piers and a height above the high tide of 60+ feet was required to serve the existing shipping channel. The concrete segmental bridge type was eliminated; the remaining five types were the tied arch, through arch, two-pier suspension/cable-stayed, four-pier extradosed, and the wave frame (see Chapter 3 for images). There were risks with each form, however, from cost escalation to geotechnical and in-water construction matters. Approaches and abutments, as well as location and type of piers, had to minimize any possible effects on the shallow water environment and water quality. Horizontal navigational clearance affected bridge choices. Overall, it had to have a minimal impact on the navigational use of the river. The Coast Guard and Army Corps of Engineers also had to approve the design and its effect. Bridge types then eliminated included the steel girder, steel box, moveable swing span, and a moveable

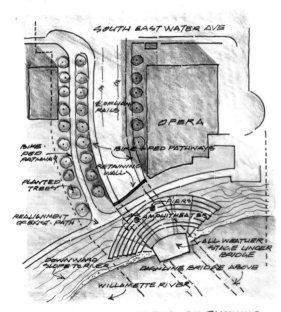

fig. 26   EAST END OF BRIDGE SHOWING AN AMPHITHEATER UNDER ON SLOPED SHORE LINE

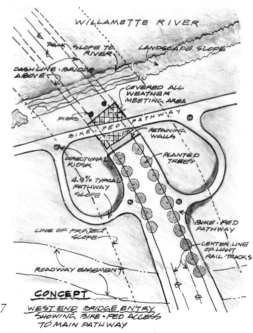

fig. 27   WEST END BRIDGE ENTRY SHOWING BIKE PED ACCESS TO MAIN PATHWAY

vertical lift.

At the end of the process there were three choices: cable-stayed, a hybrid structure combining a cable-stayed with a suspension bridge, and a wave-form truss bridge on which the truss tops when viewed horizontally would show a wave shape. The hybrid would cost $30 million more than any budget allowed. The wave-form bridge was rejected because it was a two-girder bridge that would have required complex welding in the field. It was also too expensive.

Initially, the committee examined the best features of all three, although each had issues. For example, the four-pier hybrid suspension/cable-stayed type assumed two in-water

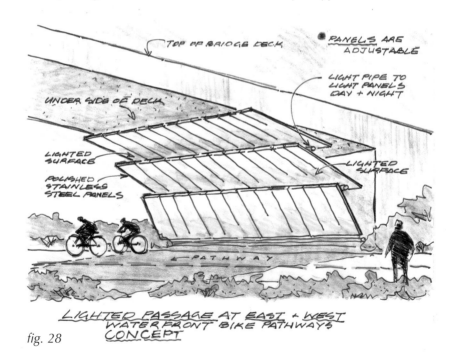

fig. 28

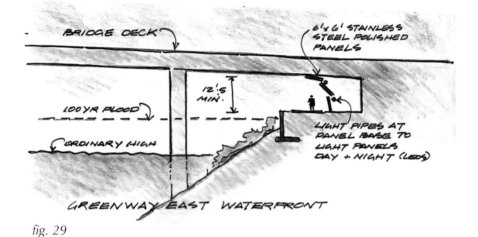

BRIDGE DECK

6'x 6' STAINLESS STEEL POLISHED PANELS

12'5 MIN.

100 YR FLOOD

ORDINARY HIGH

LIGHT PIPES AT PANEL BASE TO LIGHT PANELS DAY + NIGHT (LEDS)

GREENWAY EAST WATERFRONT

fig. 29

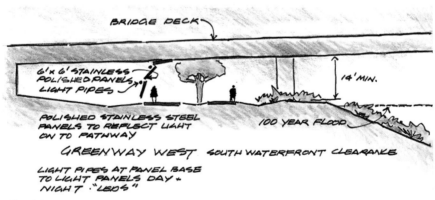

BRIDGE DECK

6'x 6' STAINLESS POLISHED PANELS LIGHT PIPES

14' MIN.

POLISHED STAINLESS STEEL PANELS TO REFLECT LIGHT ON TO PATHWAY

100 YEAR FLOOD

GREENWAY WEST SOUTH WATERFRONT CLEARANCE

LIGHT PIPES AT PANEL BASE TO LIGHT PANELS DAY + NIGHT "LEDS"

fig. 30

piers and two land piers, necessitating a greater footprint in the water and on land. There were also risks associated with each bridge type, risks involving construction, cost inflation, schedule, and design uncertainties. To clarify the aesthetics, however, renderings were created to place examples of each type across the river. The drawings included views from a distance, from the water, and from the greenway, as well as from and on and near the bridge.

The process of consultation took approximately eight months. The committee made a recommendation based on the following criteria: cost, construction risk, navigation (both width and clearance), seismic performance, architectural form, maintenance, urban context, greenway impact, and environmental sustainability, among others. The result was a systematic narrowing down of types with the committee and suggestion by Donald MacDonald, recommending a cable-stayed bridge at his first meeting with the advisory panel for the light-rail project linking Portland and the suburb of Milwaukie. Robert Hastings was again instrumental in conveying MacDonald's ideas to the board and the

entire team. The new concept was presented to the public in early 2009, at the same time the Willamette River Bridge Advisory Committee made a formal presentation to the Portland-Milwaukie Light Rail Project Steering Committee. Design development occurred with Donald MacDonald during the Preliminary Architecture and Engineering phase, 2009–10. Construction of the bridge began in 2011, and was completed in 2015. The Orange Line opened on September 12, 2015.

One of the most important consultative groups was the Portland Bicycle Transportation Alliance, now named The Street Trust, which was focused on conceptual details such as the pathway markings, textures, safety lighting, and how bicycle handlebars would work with the handrails and the exposed cables (Fig. 31).

Geographically, the new bridge would eliminate the need for southeast riders to go across the Hawthorne Bridge and then cut over to Portland State University. Of critical importance was the width of the bike lanes balanced with the pedestrian lanes. The final widths were 7 feet 8 inches for the entire length

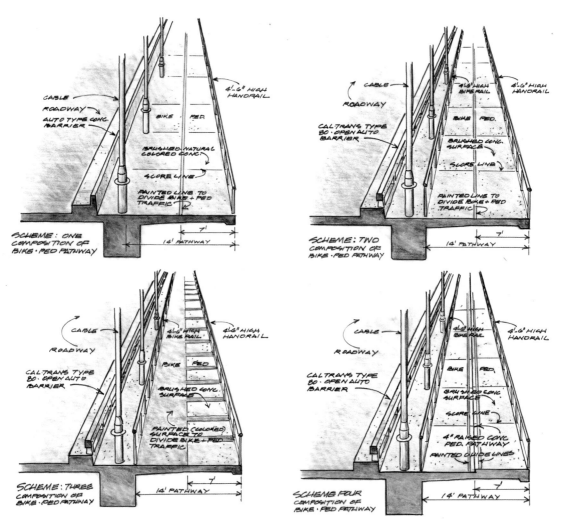

Scheme One

CABLE
ROADWAY
AUTO TYPE CONC. BARRIER
BIKE · PED.
BRUSHED NATURAL COLORED CONC.
SCORE LINE
PAINTED LINE TO DIVIDE BIKE + PED TRAFFIC
4'-6" HIGH HANDRAIL

SCHEME: ONE
COMPOSITION OF BIKE · PED PATHWAY
7'
14' PATHWAY

Scheme Two

CABLE
ROADWAY
CALTRANS TYPE 80 · OPEN AUTO BARRIER
4'-6" HIGH BIKE RAIL
4'-6" HIGH HANDRAIL
BIKE · PED.
BRUSHED CONC. SURFACE
SCORE LINE
PAINTED LINE TO DIVIDE BIKE + PED TRAFFIC

SCHEME: TWO
COMPOSITION OF BIKE · PED PATHWAY
7'
14' PATHWAY

Scheme Three

CABLE
ROADWAY
CALTRANS TYPE 80 · OPEN AUTO BARRIER
4'-6" HIGH BIKE RAIL
4'-6" HIGH HANDRAIL
BIKE · PED.
BRUSHED CONC. SURFACE
PAINTED (COLORED) SURFACE TO DIVIDE BIKE + PED TRAFFIC

SCHEME: THREE
COMPOSITION OF BIKE · PED PATHWAY
7'
14' PATHWAY

Scheme Four

CABLE
ROADWAY
CALTRANS TYPE 80 · OPEN AUTO BARRIER
4'-6" HIGH BIKE RAIL
4'-6" HIGH HANDRAIL
BIKE · PED.
BRUSHED CONC. SURFACE
SCORE LINE
4" RAISED CONC. PED. PATHWAY
PAINTED GUIDE LINES

SCHEME FOUR
COMPOSITION OF BIKE · PED PATHWAY
7'
14' PATHWAY

fig. 31

of the bridge for bikers; the walking path is 6 feet 4 inches ballooning to 13 feet 4 inches at the belvedere viewing sections next to the tower legs of the main span. There are also bike-only traffic signals on the approaches to the bridge, and the bicycle signal operates via a sensor loop embedded in the concrete; there is no need to hit a button. There are also two bicycle trip counters, one for each direction. The bike path itself is physically separated from the pedestrian walkway at the approach to the bridge to reinforce where people are to walk and bike.

The aesthetics of the bridge were fundamental to the bikers, and early riders praised the angled, unpainted stainless steel handrails and guardrails juxtaposed with the tubular white cables that stretch up the towers. Caution signs also do not litter the bridge; only what is essential for safety is there. Large green circles with the silhouette of a biker in white against a black background clearly mark the cyclists' path; pedestrian symbols consist of a large yellow circle surrounding the silhouette of a walker against a similar black background. A new covered bike parking area, bikeway network signage, and new crossing features complemented the final implementation of the bike portion of the bridge.

The advisory committee, with TriMet, recommended a cable-stayed form with two towers limited to 180 feet from the top of the pile caps. No struts would link the two columns of each tower above the deck level, which were to be modified pentagons in shape. Cable-stayed structures are usually light and somewhat flexible because of the seismic activity of the region. They also have shallow superstructures and can be constructed easily using a balanced-cantilever approach. This has a minimal effect on the waterway. To help stabilize the bridge, the committee recommended foundations as deep as 180 feet (Fig. 32).

TriMet's efforts ensured that objects and obstructions would be less likely later in the design and build phase. This even helped financially, since input reduced costs. The original budget estimate was $134 million. Final cost of the completed project was $127 million.

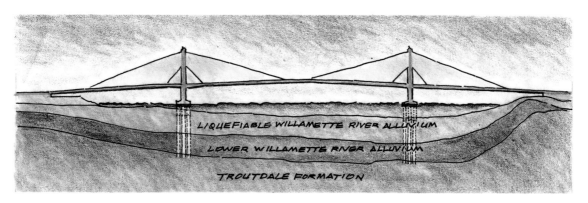

GEOTECHNICAL SOIL PROFILE

LIQUEFIABLE WILLAMETTE RIVER ALLUVIUM

LOWER WILLAMETTE RIVER ALLUVIUM

TROUTDALE FORMATION

fig. 32

At this point, TriMet with Donald MacDonald Architects proceeded to develop the bridge type and design appearance once the decision was made for a cable-stayed form. A variety of public and advisory committee consultations continued to redesign the overall form and its approaches. The following figures are the result of these consultation meetings (Figs. 33–45).

The elements of the bridge applied to soften the geometry of the cable-stayed form, extended to the outlooks around the towers, tied into the towers' form and their base.

During this process a final request for qualifications and an RFP (request for proposal) from design/build teams was prepared. By January 2010, the request went out from TriMet for qualifications with HNTB presenting preliminary engineering to roughly 30% of completion and cost estimates for the design/build construct. The bridge was to have four piers, two on land and two as towers in the water. The bridge would also include two 14-foot-wide paths for cyclists and pedestrians, one on either side of the two transit lanes.

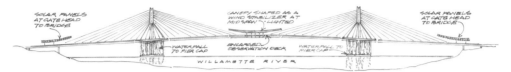

SOLAR PANELS AT GATEHEAD TO BRIDGE

CANOPY SHAPED AS A WIND STABILIZER AT MID-SPAN LIGHTED

SOLAR PANELS AT GATE HEAD TO BRIDGE

WATERFALL TO PIER CAP

ENLARGED OBSERVATION DECK

WATERFALL TO PIER CAP

WILLAMETTE RIVER

SOUTH ELEVATION OF BRIDGE SHOWING AMENITIES (GATEWAY)

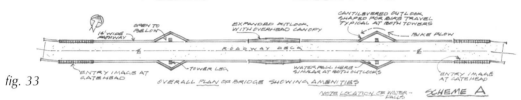

fig. 33

GREEN TO BELOW

14' WIDE PATHWAY

EXPANDED OUTLOOK WITH OVERHEAD CANOPY

CANTILEVERED OUTLOOK SHAPED FOR BIKE TRAVEL TYPICAL AT BOTH TOWERS

BIKE PLOW

ROADWAY DECK

ENTRY IMAGE AT GATEHEAD

TOWER LEG

WATERFALL HERE SIMILAR AT BOTH OUTLOOKS

ENTRY IMAGE AT GATEHEAD

OVERALL PLAN OF BRIDGE SHOWING AMENITIES

NOTE LOCATION OF WATERFALLS

SCHEME A

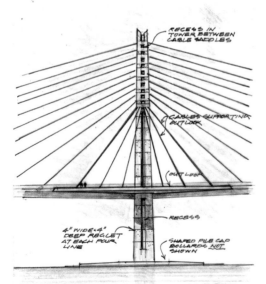

RECESS IN TOWER BETWEEN CABLE SADDLES

CABLES SUPPORTING OUTLOOK

OUTLOOK

4" WIDE × 4" DEEP REGLET AT EACH FOUR LINE

RECESS

SHAPED PILE CAP BOLLARDS NOT SHOWN

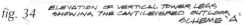

fig. 34 ELEVATION OF VERTICAL TOWER LEGS SHOWING THE CANTILEVERED OUTLOOK SCHEME 'A'

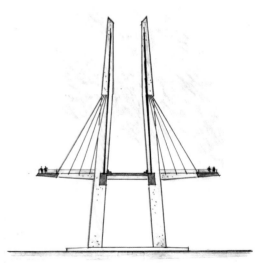

SECTION THRU DECK AT TOWER/OUTLOOK 'GATEWAY' SCHEME 'A'

VIEW OF CANTILEVERED OUTLOOK AT TOWER
SIMILAR AT BOTH SIDES OF EACH TOWER
(NOTE: VERTICAL TOWER LEGS)   SCHEME 'A'

fig. 35

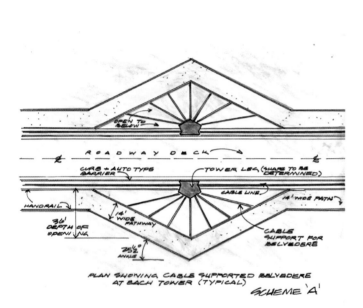

OPEN TO BELOW

ROADWAY DECK

CURB + AUTO TYPE BARRIER

TOWER LEG (SHAPE TO BE DETERMINED)

CABLE LINE

14' WIDE PATH

HANDRAIL

14' WIDE PATHWAY

36' DEPTH OF OPENING

25½° ANGLE

CABLE SUPPORT FOR BELVEDERE

PLAN SHOWING CABLE SUPPORTED BELVEDERE AT EACH TOWER (TYPICAL)   SCHEME 'A'

fig. 36

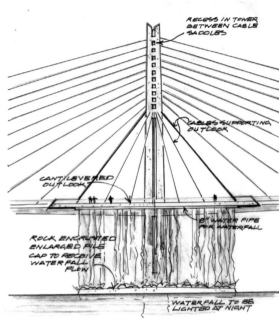

RECESS IN TOWER BETWEEN CABLE SADDLES

CABLES SUPPORTING OUTLOOK

CANTILEVERED OUTLOOK

8" WATER PIPE FOR WATERFALL

ROCK ENCRUSTED ENLARGED PILE CAP TO RECEIVE WATERFALL FLOW

WATERFALL TO BE LIGHTED AT NIGHT

ELEVATION OF CANTED VERTICAL TOWER LEGS SHOWING WATERFALL FROM OVERLOOK

SCHEME 'A'

fig. 37

Additionally, the bridge would be 75.5 feet wide except at the towers, where it would widen to 110.5 feet so the paths for pedestrians and cyclists could curve around the towers and also allow for an open space between the towers and the pathways. Initially, ten cables would extend from either side of each of the towers in a semi-fan arrangement.

One of the considerations in these studies was wind, since winds near the river and in the Columbia River valley are of significant concern. Various wind tunnels tested designs. Bridge dynamics were also important because cable-supported bridge decks are flexible, but pedestrians and others had to feel secure. Trains, buses, and streetcars rolling on a bridge push the structure, so to ensure pedestrian ease, a so-called "rolling stock" analysis was done to verify that there would be no "excitation" to the bridge from the mass transit vehicles for passengers, bikers, or pedestrians.

One other important feature was the ability of the bridge to support special loading: on certain occasions such as holidays or festivals, transit would be suspended to allow pedestrians only. Could the bridge support the live load and not create excessive response? Analysis confirmed that the bridge could support live load of pedestrians on both sides in the event of a larger gathering of people.

By May 2010, TriMet selected three firms to proceed to the design/build contract stage. Interviews and discussions with the three firms followed, continuing until September 2010. This was a two-stage process, first a request for qualifications and then the design/build stage, important in the final selection based on cost and technical proposals as well as design elements received in October 2010. The chosen design/build team was Kiewit of Omaha, Nebraska, as primary contractor and T.Y. Lin as primary engineer.

A critical component, emphasized in the many public meetings, was schedule. If the bridge got behind schedule, the 7.3-mile light-rail Orange Line from Northern Clackamas County to downtown Portland would be impacted. The design/build proposal did not allow for any change above water to the appearance approved by TriMet through

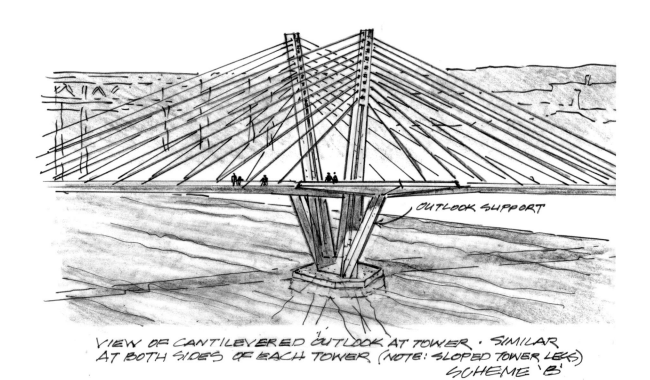

OUTLOOK SUPPORT

VIEW OF CANTILEVERED OUTLOOK AT TOWER · SIMILAR
AT BOTH SIDES OF EACH TOWER (NOTE: SLOPED TOWER LEGS)
SCHEME 'B'

fig. 38

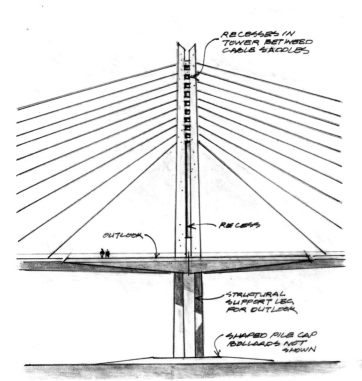

RECESSES IN TOWER BETWEEN CABLE SADDLES

RECESS

OUTLOOK

STRUCTURAL SUPPORT LEG FOR OUTLOOK

SHAPED PILE CAP BOLLARDS NOT SHOWN

ELEVATION OF SLOPED TOWER LEGS SHOWING THE CANTILEVERED OUTLOOK SCHEME 'B'

fig. 39

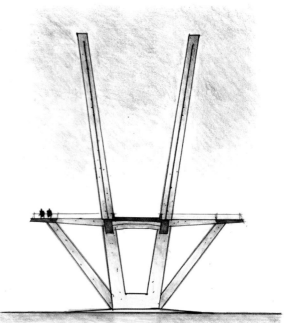

SECTION THRU DECK AT TOWER/OUTLOOK SCHEME 'B'

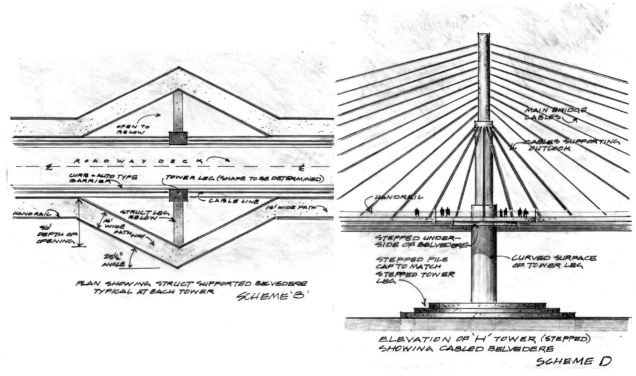

PLAN SHOWING STRUCT SUPPORTED BELVEDERE
TYPICAL AT EACH TOWER

SCHEME 'B'

fig. 40

ELEVATION OF 'H' TOWER (STEPPED)
SHOWING CABLED BELVEDERE

SCHEME D

fig. 41

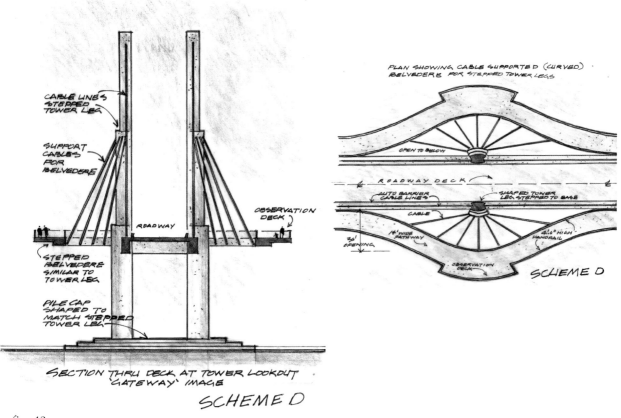

CABLE LINES
STEPPED
TOWER LEG

SUPPORT
CABLES
FOR
BELVEDERE

OBSERVATION
DECK

ROADWAY

STEPPED
BELVEDERE
SIMILAR TO
TOWER LEG

PILE CAP
SHAPED TO
MATCH STEPPED
TOWER LEG

SECTION THRU DECK AT TOWER LOOKOUT
'GATEWAY' IMAGE

SCHEME D

PLAN SHOWING CABLE SUPPORTED (CURVED)
BELVEDERE FOR STEPPED TOWER LEGS

OPEN TO BELOW

ROADWAY DECK

AUTO BARRIER
CABLE LINES

SHAPED TOWER
LEG STEPPED TO BASE

CABLE

14' WIDE
PATHWAY

4'6" HIGH
HANDRAIL

30'
OPENING

OBSERVATION
DECK

SCHEME D

fig. 42

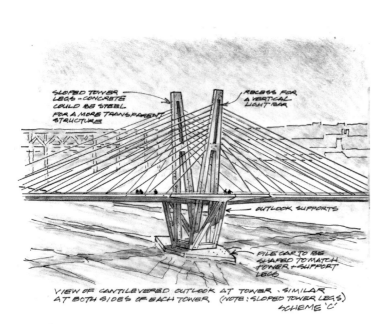

SLOPED TOWER
LEGS - CONCRETE
COULD BE STEEL
FOR A MORE TRANSPARENT
STRUCTURE

RECESS FOR
A VERTICAL
LIGHT BAR

OUTLOOK SUPPORTS

PILE CAP TO BE
SHAPED TO MATCH
TOWER + SUPPORT
LEGS

VIEW OF CANTILEVERED OUTLOOK AT TOWER, SIMILAR
AT BOTH SIDES OF EACH TOWER. (NOTE: SLOPED TOWER LEGS)
SCHEME 'C'

fig. 43

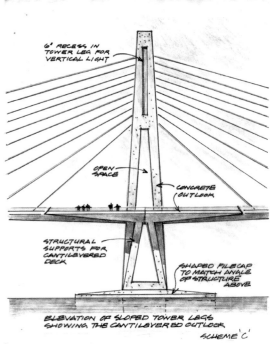

6" RECESS IN
TOWER LEG FOR
VERTICAL LIGHT

OPEN
SPACE

CONCRETE
OUTLOOK

STRUCTURAL
SUPPORTS FOR
CANTILEVERED
DECK

SHAPED PILECAP
TO MATCH ANGLE
OF STRUCTURE
ABOVE

ELEVATION OF SLOPED TOWER LEGS
SHOWING THE CANTILEVERED OUTLOOK

SCHEME 'C'

fig. 44

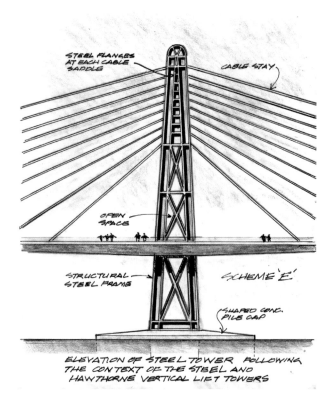

STEEL FLANGES
AT EACH CABLE
SADDLE

CABLE STAY

OPEN
SPACE

STRUCTURAL
STEEL FRAME

SCHEME 'E'

SHAPED CONC.
PILE CAP

ELEVATION OF STEEL TOWER FOLLOWING
THE CONTEXT OF THE STEEL AND
HAWTHORNE VERTICAL LIFT TOWERS

fig. 45a

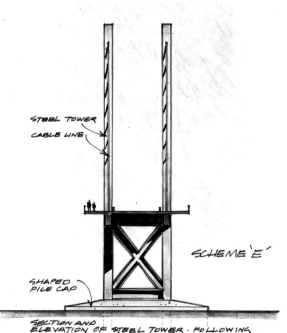

STEEL TOWER

CABLE LINE

SCHEME 'E'

SHAPED
PILE CAP

SECTION AND
ELEVATION OF STEEL TOWER · FOLLOWING
THE CONTEXT OF THE STEEL AND HAWTHORNE
VERTICAL LIFT TOWERS

fig. 45b

public participation or primary members of the bridge. All construction drawings were checked by MacDonald Architects for compliance with TriMet and public input. These requirements were essential to meet the construction deadline.

A series of further consultations occurred with TriMet holding hearings, peer review panels, public and client reviews involving all the stakeholders. Landscape architects, as well as biologists concerned with river life, were also consulted.

One of the challenges to address were sea lions, which come upstream in their hunt for salmon. They frequently stayed on the pile caps under the other bridges along the river but here needed a deterrence. The hearings brought about some potential solutions to the problem (Figs. 46 & 47). One of the solutions was intensive planting on top of the pile caps ranging from shrubs to small plants, supported by a stainless steel mesh held up over the concrete pile caps that also ran below the water. In the end, the pile caps were modified and sloped to address the issue of sea lions.

TriMet staff, engineers, architects, the design community, peer review committee, and contractors continued to play a role. The general consensus was for something simple

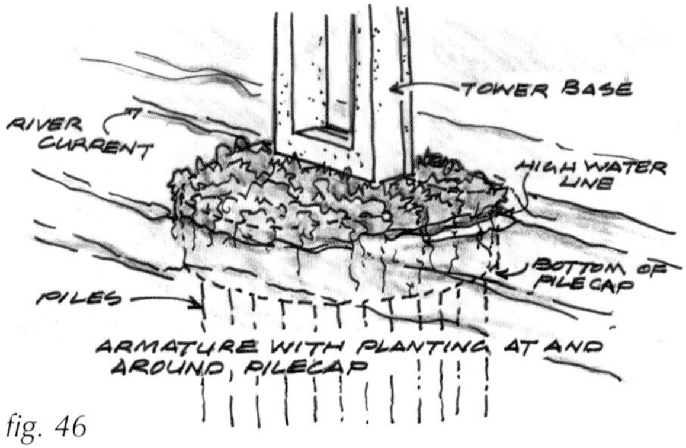

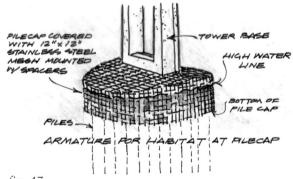

fig. 46

fig. 47

and beautiful.

Despite the details outlined by TriMet and HNTB, choices had to be made, as the following set of drawings indicate. They range from the design and placement of wind stabilizers to cable schemes for the cantilevered outlook, tower design with cable saddles broken into segments to maintain scale, an observation deck at mid-span—not built—bike paths, pedestrian walkways, and even the touchdown near the South Portland medical center.

The tower forms took on a particular shape,

largely in an effort to blend scale and design.

Even the angle wind fairing element below the handrail repeats the tower angles cut to match the tree line in the distance. The wind fairings also emphasize the chevron form found even on the angles of the tower leg, echoing MacDonald's principle that a successful bridge evolves out of the context of its place and community. A successful bridge must be a natural part of the environment. MacDonald also tried to relate, or echo, the form with the other existing steel bridges on the river, the low towers recommended by the advisory panel, maintaining the aesthetic not just of the bridge

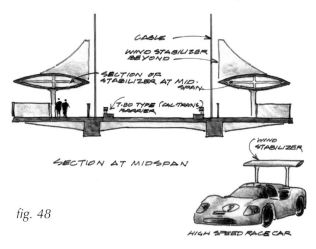

fig. 48

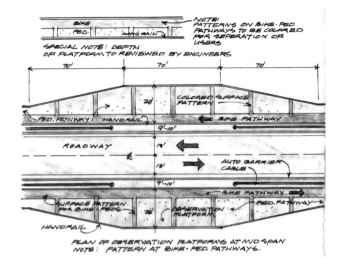

fig. 49

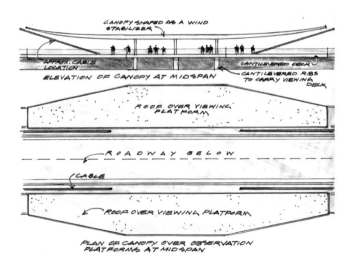

fig. 50

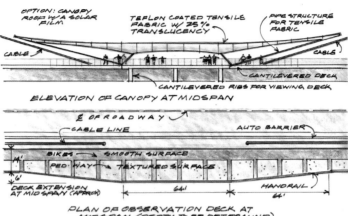

OPTION: CANOPY ROOF W/ A SOLAR FILM

TEFLON COATED TENSILE FABRIC W/ 25% TRANSLUCENCY

PIPE STRUCTURE FOR TENSILE FABRIC.

CABLE

CABLE

CANTILEVERED DECK

CANTILEVERED RIBS FOR VIEWING DECK

ELEVATION OF CANOPY AT MIDSPAN

℄ OF ROADWAY

CABLE LINE

AUTO BARRIER

BIKES — SMOOTH SURFACE

PED' WAY — TEXTURED SURFACE

14'

6'

DECK EXTENSION AT MIDSPAN (APPROX)

64'

HANDRAIL

64'

PLAN OF OBSERVATION DECK AT MIDSPAN (DEPTH TO BE DETERMIND)

MIDSPAN OBSERVATION DECK

fig. 51

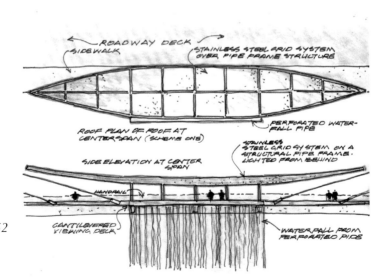

ROADWAY DECK

SIDEWALK

STAINLESS STEEL GRID SYSTEM OVER PIPE FRAME STRUCTURE

PERFORATED WATER-FALL PIPE

ROOF PLAN OF ROOF AT CENTERSPAN (SCHEME ONE)

STAINLESS STEEL GRID SYSTEM ON A STRUCTURAL PIPE FRAME. LIGHTED FROM BEHIND

SIDE ELEVATION AT CENTER SPAN

HANDRAIL

CANTILEVERED VIEWING DECK

WATERFALL FROM PERFORATED PIPE

fig. 52

73

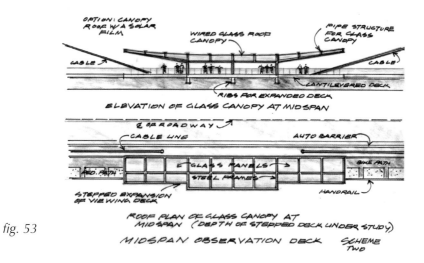

OPTION: CANOPY ROOF W/ A SOLAR FILM

WIRED GLASS ROOF CANOPY

PIPE STRUCTURE FOR GLASS CANOPY

CABLE

CABLE

CANTILEVERED DECK

RIBS FOR EXPANDED DECK

ELEVATION OF GLASS CANOPY AT MIDSPAN

℄ OF ROADWAY

CABLE LINE

AUTO BARRIER

PED. PATH

GLASS PANELS

STEEL FRAMES

BIKE PATH

STEPPED EXPANSION OF VIEWING DECK

HANDRAIL

fig. 53

ROOF PLAN OF GLASS CANOPY AT MIDSPAN (DEPTH OF STEPPED DECK UNDER STUDY)

MIDSPAN OBSERVATION DECK   SCHEME TWO

form but of the existing landscape, bridges, and visibility.

Stability remains a persistent challenge with cable-stayed bridges, and one response was to add a form to ensure stability. The first idea was a wing, similar to that on race cars (Fig. 48).

Various materials were proposed, from Teflon to glass, aluminum, and steel shaped like an airplane wing. At one point the wing was to be integrated with a waterfall at the outlooks that surrounded the two towers. (Figs. 49–53).

In the end, however, the wing was not built. Stability was achieved through the three-foot sloped deck edging, which acted as a wind faring. Also, the cable stay bundle covering has an integral helixrib on its exterior. This rib helps reduce the vibration of the cables in high wind and helped shed rain. When rain hits a cable without the helix wrapping, it increases vibration. And to eliminate swaying or shaking when bikes, pedestrians, and mass transit were simultaneously on the bridge, special positioning of the tower cables, splayed outward with special cable saddles at the top, was initiated. Normally a cable-stayed system would have cable connections in the hollow legs of the superstructure, the process of cable stressing occurring at both ends from inside the tower leg to the deck. Tilikum Crossing, however, became the first bridge in the United States to use a multi-tube saddle design that enabled each cable to run continuously from the deck through the top of the tower and back down to the other side of the deck. Approximately 3.5 miles of cable run continuously through the tower saddle, instead of terminating in each tower. The stressing of the stay cables is performed at the deck level and carried out simultaneously at both ends. And because tubes of polyethylene cover the cables, they are protected from the elements. Additionally, constructing the bridge out of concrete rather than steel ensured the minimization of vibration and low maintenance (Fig. 54).

Of course, neighborhoods matter. And Portland, like other American cities, has seen its industrial neighborhoods transition to a mix of residential and commercial use. To the west of

Tilikum Crossing is now the South Waterfront district, earlier a shipyard; to the east, Tilikum Crossing touches down in the former industrial Central Eastside district, part of which is being rezoned for mixed-use development. The need to connect these changing areas was evident, although neither neighborhood had the road infrastructure to support the increased traffic that would have come with an additional auto bridge. Instead, Tilikum Crossing was conceived first and foremost as a conduit for a light-rail line and a centerpiece for this new district in Portland.

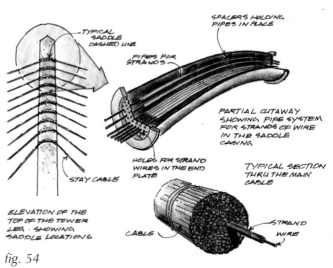

fig. 54

Tilikum Crossing was to be more than a bridge but an element to brand the city for the 21st century. Consequently, it needed a geometry and a form that could last 100 years, as have other great bridges in America such as the Brooklyn Bridge, the Golden Gate, or Lions Gate (Vancouver, British Columbia, Canada). The form could be not subjective but timeless, achieved through mathematics. In short, one builds an elegant piece of geometry (Fig. 55).

Hence the decision to eliminate cars and trucks, allowing for a narrower and even more graceful structure. The impact of the resulting form can be measured by the use of a photograph of the bridge on the cover of the United States Department of Transportation's proposed budget booklet for 2016.

To enhance the build process involved the use of two simultaneous computer models to maintain quality and accuracy through each construction phase. Kiewit/ TY Lin and HNTB ran the two models simultaneously, which allowed the contractor's engineer and the owner's engineer to compare results of each construction segment. This system allowed accurate bridge geometry control, including

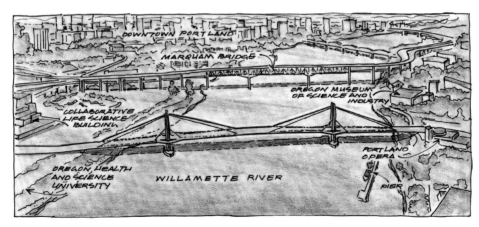

fig. 55

VIEW SHOWING FINAL CONSTRUCTION AND CONTEXT OF TILIKUM CROSSING (2015)

a 5% grade limit set by the Americans with Disabilities Act.

South of Portland's numerous Willamette crossings, the area for Tilikum Crossing lacked an existing road infrastructure to accommodate a new vehicle-heavy bridge. Consequently, the idea of a no-car bridge emerged, and because there was no need to accommodate four or six lanes of vehicle traffic, the bridge could be narrow (Fig. 56).

Additional challenges were several critical utility lines, notably a water main, gas line, and high-pressure gas line beneath the riverbed.

The final design embodies the elegance of geometry with the practicality of social and transportation needs. It does so in three ways: minimal intrusion on the environment, incorporation of its natural context, and use of materials that have a minimal impact on the

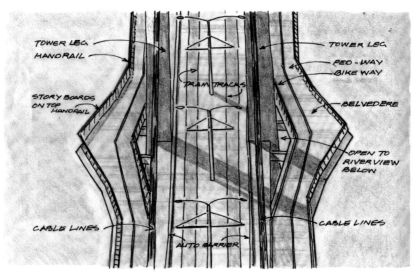

fig. 56   BIRD'S EYE VIEW OVERLOOKING THE EXTENDED BELVEDERES AT THE TOWER

natural life of the river, tied together into an expressive form. Even construction reflected these concerns, since work in the river had to occur during a four-month window that opened only once a year for the benefit of fish migration.

The long main span deck is separated into a 31-foot-wide transit way between the tower legs to accommodate two lanes of track and two flanking multiuse paths for pedestrians and cyclists (Fig. 57).

Lacking wide automobile on-ramps, the bridge is able to fit pedestrian and bike paths on both sides (the few large all-vehicular bridges that allow foot traffic have such paths on one side only). MacDonald fashioned these paths so that they jut outward at the bridge's towers, leaving empty spaces between the paths and the main bridge.

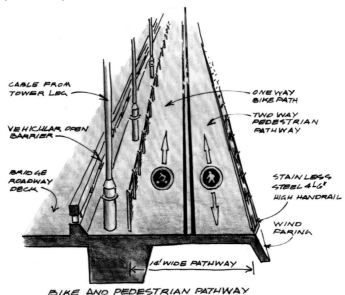

fig. 57

CABLE FROM TOWER LEG

VEHICULAR OPEN BARRIER

BRIDGE ROADWAY DECK

ONE WAY BIKE PATH

TWO WAY PEDESTRIAN PATHWAY

STAINLESS STEEL 4'6" HIGH HANDRAIL

WIND FARING

14' WIDE PATHWAY

BIKE AND PEDESTRIAN PATHWAY 'ON BOTH SIDES OF BRIDGE'

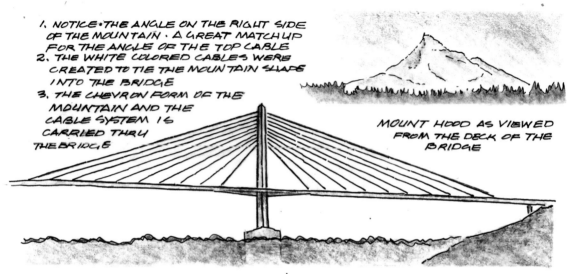

1. NOTICE·THE ANGLE ON THE RIGHT SIDE OF THE MOUNTAIN·A GREAT MATCH UP FOR THE ANGLE OR THE TOP CABLE
2. THE WHITE COLORED CABLES WERE CREATED TO TIE THE MOUNTAIN SHAPE INTO THE BRIDGE
3. THE CHEVRON FORM OF THE MOUNTAIN AND THE CABLE SYSTEM IS CARRIED THRU THE BRIDGE

MOUNT HOOD AS VIEWED FROM THE DECK OF THE BRIDGE

THE ELEVATION OF THE BRIDGE'S TYPICAL TOWERS AND CABLE SYSTEM

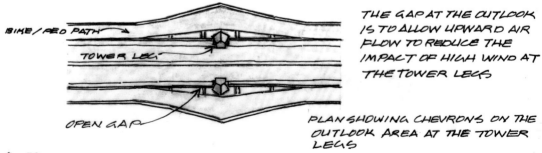

BIKE/PED PATH

TOWER LEG

OPEN GAP

THE GAP AT THE OUTLOOK IS TO ALLOW UPWARD AIR FLOW TO REDUCE THE IMPACT OF HIGH WIND AT THE TOWER LEGS

PLAN SHOWING CHEVRONS ON THE OUTLOOK AREA AT THE TOWER LEGS

fig. 58

The shorter H-shaped towers and intricate geometrical shape put stress on concrete construction for the tower legs' infrastructure. Building a slender bridge without soaring towers resulted in tighter tolerances for loading the concrete, which required 78 cast-in-place bridge segments each with an exacting 577-page construction manual (Popular Mechanics, August 20, 2015).

The pentagon form relates to the golden triangle concept in geometry, an isosceles triangle in which the duplicated side is in the golden ratio to the distinct side.

The chevron shape for the cables dictates the forms on the deck as aesthetics and geometry unite. The chevron form earlier appeared on the Golden Gate Bridge in San Francisco as an element to tie in the disparate parts of the structure and reinforce the overall composition of the form. For Tilikum Crossing, the chevron form of Mount Hood, the cables, and the tower legs with a chevron form on the outside unify the bridge elements. Additionally, the pop-out of the outlooks around the twin towers reinforces the tower shadows that come off the handrails and display a chevron form at certain times of day. The shadow of the cables on the bridge deck displays a chevron form, echoing the half chevrons on the tower tops (Fig. 58).

Even the underside of the bridge possesses form, specifically that of a cathedral. The bottom of the bridge exhibits a cathedral-type ceiling that encloses the conduits and services. The use of a clean underside free of conduits on Tilikum Crossing provides an architecturally defined ceiling, a unique vernacular establishing a visually pleasing form from above and below, especially for boats passing beneath the bridge (Fig. 59).

Of particular importance to emphasize the height and elegance of the towers is that the tower legs slope inward as they ascend. This is partly because the lens in the eye is convex, which widens the image at the top as you look up, a technique used in the shaping of the Parthenon in Greece. If the towers went straight up without any adjustment, they would appear to expand and look out of proportion to the cables and remainder of the bridge.

UNDERSIDE OF BRIDGE DECK TREATED AS A
CATHEDRAL TYPE CEILING WITH MINIMAL
INTRUSION OF EXPOSED PIPES AND CONDUITS

fig. 59

Sloping inward while moving upward corrects the retina as it views the object. The tower legs actually taper inward from a diameter of 16 feet at the base to 9 feet at the top. This makes the towers look outward and larger because they taper inward. The play with perspective also makes the towers appear parallel to each other, but only because they tilt inward, making them look taller.

The chevron form aids in making the towers look thinner because light hits the soloed section of the pentagon, creating shadows on the open side, making the other look thinner because of the light. The overall effect is to create a thinner bridge, at least in appearance. Even the surfaces of the pile caps take on a chevron form, formed partly to deter sea lions from residing. Form also echoes the prow of a boat; even the wind fairings on the bridge are in the shape of a half chevron, also incorporated in the form of the connectors needed to hold the trolley lines. Importantly, the chevron functions structurally and aesthetically to harmonize the form of the bridge itself and its environment (Figs. 60 & 61).

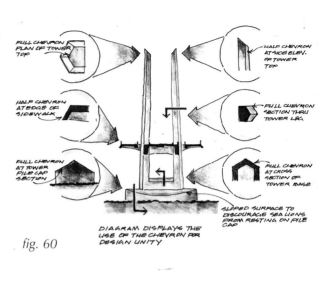

fig. 60

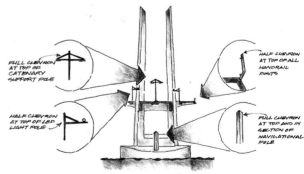

fig. 61

A critical design feature for Tilikum Crossing is the rule of thirds, found in art, architecture, and photography. This means one does not divide the horizon in half but into thirds, the segments offering a better, more varied sense of form. Removing the center as the focal point creates visual and even structural interest. The eye investigates and even contributes to shaping the work. The viewer becomes active, not passive (Figs. 62 & 63).

Even the pile caps and shafts for the tower base tie in with the overall form of the bridge, especially the use of the chevron form. Originally, there was to be a circular pile cap, which then became an oval form. But it ties in with the vocabulary of the bridge, adjusted to reflect a chevron form. The top of the pile cap was also sloped. Even the navigational lights on the pile caps express the chevron form (Fig. 64).

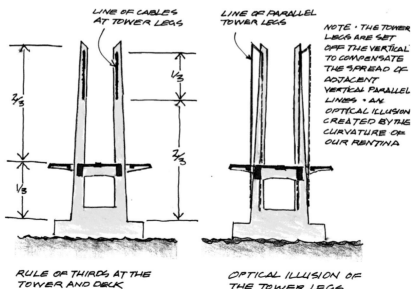

LINE OF CABLES
AT TOWER LEGS

2/3

1/3

LINE OF PARALLEL
TOWER LEGS

1/3

2/3

NOTE · THE TOWER LEGS ARE SET OFF THE VERTICAL TO COMPENSATE THE SPREAD OF ADJACENT VERTICAL PARALLEL LINES · AN OPTICAL ILLUSION CREATED BY THE CURVATURE OF OUR RETINA

fig. 62

RULE OF THIRDS AT THE
TOWER AND DECK

OPTICAL ILLUSION OF
THE TOWER LEGS

fig. 63

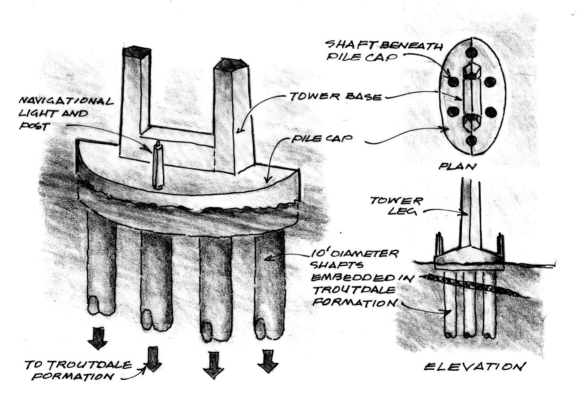

SHAFT BENEATH PILE CAP

TOWER BASE

PLAN

TOWER LEG

ELEVATION

NAVIGATIONAL LIGHT AND POST

PILE CAP

10' DIAMETER SHAFTS EMBEDDED IN TROUTDALE FORMATION

TO TROUTDALE FORMATION

TYPICAL PILE CAP AND SHAFTS FOR TOWER BASE

fig. 64

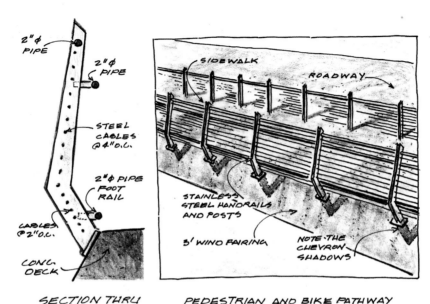

SECTION THRU HANDRAIL

fig. 65

PEDESTRIAN AND BIKE PATHWAY HANDRAILS WITH MID-MORNING CHEVRON SHADOWS

An additional element that incorporates the overall design language are the handrails. They slope inward to prevent anyone from climbing on them, with their shape in the sunlight also offering a chevron shadow while the slope of the wind fairings also repeats half the tower leg, but more importantly, breaks up the wind. Without them, a vacuum would be created that would likely create oscillation of the deck. The newly designed fairings are stable up to winds of 150 miles per hour. Shadows in fact play an important part of the overall design, the light at different hours altering shapes and forms. Even the cabling at the top of the tower legs ties in with the top of the handrail forming a half chevron (Fig. 65).

Other unique features include acoustical reflector dishes integrated into each of the bridge abutments created by the San Francisco artists Anna Valentina Murch and Douglas Hollis, the design team artists who also designed the aesthetic lighting on the bridge. Each of these artistic elements is 24 x 12 feet in the shape of a parabolic reflector covered in custom made, one-inch stainless steel penny tiles. Sounds bounce off the reflector when people stand in a certain place marked on the pathway, making it an interactive art work. The lighting for the dishes also changes color and motion depending on the natural conditions of the river, since they are tied into the lighting system.

One rejected idea was the creation of a sonic bike path, a sequence of concrete grooves on the path that would play "59th Street Bridge Song (Feelin' Groovy)" by Simon and Garfunkel. Concerns with cost, safety, and design ended the idea. The grooves would sing out along the last 150 feet of each end of the bridge as cyclists leave the span. "Slow down, you move too fast" would be the key refrain. But the project would have cost over $200,000, simply too much for the budget.

Light, both natural and electrical, becomes a significant design element—as the next chapter will show—and, when properly treated, actually makes the overall form of the bridge appear graceful and slender.

Construction of the bridge began in January 2011 and was completed in August 2014. A year later, systems, signaling, and operational work was finalized. Marking the popularity of the bridge is Portland's bike barometer, which measures bike crossings on the Hawthorne and Tilikum Crossing Bridges. As of 29 July 2016, there were 613,231 crossings on Tilikum Crossing.

One further important element of the final design was the name. Donald MacDonald wanted to name the bridge Rothko Bridge. The painter Mark Rothko was a colorist, and the use of color on the bridge structure is representative of his work. He also started his early career in Portland and went on to become world famous as a modern painter.

"Tilikum" is actually Chinook Wawa, an international language used by first Oregonians and later spoken by explorers, fur traders, settlers, and the first few generations of Portlanders. (In fact, it's still spoken today!) Tilikum means "people," "tribe," and "relatives" and has come to describe friendly people and friends.

The Bridge Naming Committee reviewed nearly 9,500 submissions in their highly publicized naming contest to find those that would connect and inspire—not just now, but 100 years from now—and best reflect the region's history and culture.

Committee chair and historian Chet Orloff said the Native American name was selected because it holds the "most promise to connect the people of our region today with the long past of people who have been here for thousands of years, and to connect with future generations." Furthermore, he explained that Tilikum symbolizes coming together. It conveys connections, not only in the relationships between people but in the connections we will make as we ride, walk, run, and cycle across this beautiful new bridge.

While the spelling "Tillicum" was initially proposed, the Committee selected "Tilikum" because that's how the first people who lived here spelled the word and how their descendants spell it today.

Other finalists were the Abigail Scott Duniway Bridge, the Cascadia Crossing Transit Bridge, and the Wy'east Transit Bridge.

In March 2016, however, an online prankster managed to change the official name of the so-called "Bridge of the People" on Google Maps to Jean-Luc Picard Wunder Crossing, paying tribute to the Starship Enterprise captain on Star Trek: The Next Generation.

That name was actually one of hundreds submitted by the public when the transit agency was building the bridge.

About a week after the bridge opened in September 2015, Portland business owner Owen Lingley purchased two Star Trek–themed billboards near Portland State University suggesting the very same name change.

CONVERSATION: LIGHTING, THE RIVER, AND THE BRIDGE

One of the most important and unique elements of Tilikum Crossing is the lights, incorporating 178 LED lights placed on 40 bridge cables plus the four tower legs above and below the deck, and on the Sonic Dish artwork along the Eastside Esplanade and future Willamette Greenway at the ends of the bridge. They illuminate the cables, towers, and underside of the deck. Uniquely, using special software, the lights change colors in response to the Willamette River's speed, height, and water temperature, the last determining the base color. The river's speed controls the pace the colors change and move across the bridge, while the river's height is displayed by a second color that moves vertically up and down the towers and the cables. LED lights are cheap, one-third the cost of regular mercury vapor lighting, with bulbs that last some 50,000 hours (Fig. 66).

But the bridge is also a living work of art, with lights dancing across the structure controlled by the tide. When the tide comes in, the lights move toward the center of the bridge. As the tide goes out, the lights move toward the ends of the bridge. Additionally, the tide levels affect the speed of the lights. When the tide is higher or lower, the lights move faster. At midpoint, the lights move slowly. The speed of the river controls how quickly the colors change. If the river is moving fast, the colors will appear to move and cycle through more quickly. Even temperature has a role: the cooler the temperature, the cooler the color.

Collaborating with the lighting is sound. Parabolic reflectors under the east and west ends of the bridge enhance the acoustic sound of nature. Remarkably, the amplification is passive: the parabolic shape compresses the sound to a small area, increasing loudness at the point of sound focusing by an estimated six to ten decibels. Pedestrians walking within 5 to 10 feet of the dish will be in the zone of sound, but beyond 20 feet, the sound will not be heard (Figs. 67 & 68).

More importantly, the lighting and the acoustic discs develop a conversation with the river, uniting art and science. The shifting image of the bridge responds to the science of the river, incorporating sound. The appeal is to all the senses as movement, sound, sight, and

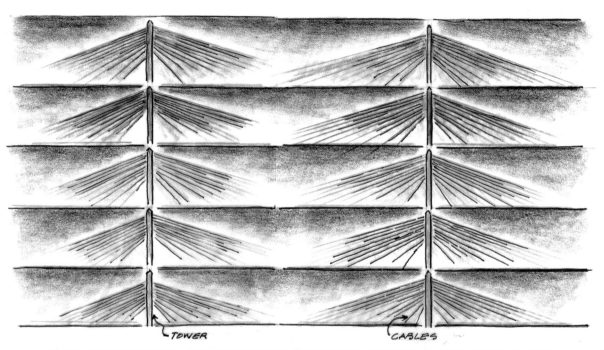

TOWER

CABLES

FULL SPECTRUM OF THE COLOR PALETTE FOR THE LED MOOD LIGHTING DESIGNED BY ANNA MURCH AND DOUG HOLLIS WITH PROGRAMMING BY MORGAN BARNARD

● LED FIXTURES BETWEEN EACH PAIR OF CABLES

fig. 66

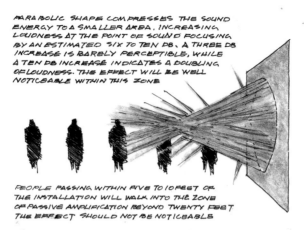

PARABOLIC SHAPE COMPRESSES THE SOUND ENERGY TO A SMALLER AREA, INCREASING LOUDNESS AT THE POINT OF SOUND FOCUSING BY AN ESTIMATED SIX TO TEN DB. A THREE DB INCREASE IS BARELY PERCEPTIBLE, WHILE A TEN DB INCREASE INDICATES A DOUBLING OF LOUDNESS. THE EFFECT WILL BE WELL NOTICEABLE WITHIN THIS ZONE

PEOPLE PASSING WITHIN FIVE TO 10 FEET OF THE INSTALLATION WILL WALK INTO THE ZONE OF PASSIVE AMPLIFICATION. BEYOND TWENTY FEET THE EFFECT SHOULD NOT BE NOTICEABLE

fig. 67

SOUND ENERY DIAGRAM FOR THE PARABOLIC ACOUSTICAL REFLECTOR

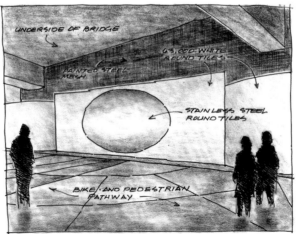

UNDERSIDE OF BRIDGE

93,000 WHITE ROUND TILES

PAINTED STEEL MESH

STAINLESS STEEL ROUND TILES

BIKE AND PEDESTRIAN PATHWAY

fig. 68

PARABOLIC ACOUSTICAL REFLECTOR UNDERNEATH THE EAST AND WEST ENDS OF THE BRIDGE

even smell contribute to the experience of the bridge. Safety lights complement the decorative lights, but it's the interaction and complexity of the two systems that establish the other unique elements of the bridge and its appearance as it becomes a living work of art.

These changing artistic values vary with the season, so in the summer (when the river levels are pretty static) the bridge color will appear even and bright. In the spring, when the water tends to move faster, the bridge colors will appear more fluid.

Although a good deal of scientific data is gathered to create the aesthetic light display, the bridge lights do not serve as a weather tool. The artists, the late Anna Valentina Murch and Douglas Hollis, wanted the lights to represent a visual dialogue between the naturalness of the Willamette River and Tilikum Crossing. Morgan Bernard was able to translate their conceptions into reality.

The software controlling these light changes essentially looks at data from the US Geological Survey river monitor near the Morrison Bridge (there are about 8,000 such

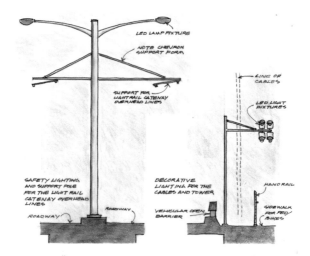

fig. 69

fig. 70

monitoring stations nationwide), transmitted to a computer via a special software program. It then processes that data and sends it to an architectural lighting control. Technically, results from lighting test measurements involving a color DNA were fed back into a color programming algorithm in an iterative process to perfect the colors for the final display.

The combination of scientific data and art creates a kaleidoscope of ever-changing colors and forms, turning the bridge into a remarkable piece of light sculpture. Lighting also has an influence on the environment, specifically on bird life and the environment. The biology of light became another concern of the light designers.

In addition to the decorative lighting is safety lighting, including lights for aviation on top of the towers and navigational lighting below. Decorative lighting is also special event lighting. Safety lighting, which ensures proper visibility for pedestrians and bikers, with LED lights illuminating pathways as well as east and west entrances to the bridge, is also important (Figs. 69–71).

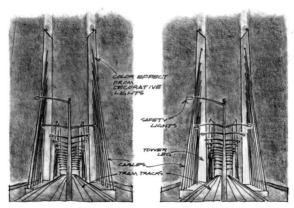

COLOR EFFECT FROM DECORATIVE LIGHTS

SAFETY LIGHTS

TOWER LEG

CABLES

TRAM TRACKS

fig. 71

DECORATIVE LIGHTING VIEW FROM EAST END OF THE BRIDGE LOOKING WEST SHOWN WITHOUT THE SAFTEY LIGHTING

SAFETY LIGHTING VIEW FROM EAST END OF THE BRIDGE LOOKING WEST SHOWING THE EFFECT OF MIXING THE TWO LIGHTING SYSTEMS

The wildlife surrounding Tilikum Crossing mixes seasonal and permanent inhabitants, features that affected some of the design elements, beginning with the salmon that move upstream to spawn. They needed to be respected both during the construction phase and after. The fish potentially affected by the sound waves from the pounding of the piles and by the turbidity of the subsoil in the new bridge construction included coho salmon, steelhead trout, sturgeon, lamprey, and cutthroat trout. But other threatened, endangered, or sensitive species in the project area include the American bald eagle, the peregrine falcon, and the purple martin; among amphibians and reptiles are the Oregon salamander, the painted turtle, and the spotted frog.

Bats are another important species, and various bridges on the Willamette are bat friendly. There are fifteen species of bats in Oregon, and approximately seven species regularly use the bridges of the Willamette. Bat habitats, in fact, are regularly included in new bridge construction.

Construction of Tilikum Crossing was sensitive to life on the river; architects and engineers realized that building this bridge had a remarkable environmental impact in terms of actual animals and nature, as well as people. Penetrating the surface of the water, mentioned above, affects the mammal life of the river. In fact, building on the river could only be done at certain periods of time, and it could not be done during migration, or spawning seasons. Construction always affects habitat during and after construction.

Below is an illustrated list of the major wildlife forms in Portland and within the construction area, bearing in mind that sometimes wildlife can be greatly disturbed by new bridge construction.

Peregrines love to nest in Portland's Willamette River bridges. There is constant monitoring of these falcons. They began to scout out the Fremont Bridge in 1993 and are also nesting on five other bridges in the area. The Willamette River's bridges have become the most productive nesting site in the state. Clocked at 200 miles an hour, peregrine falcons are considered to be the fastest birds on earth (Fig. 72).

American white pelicans are large birds and mostly colored white. The American white pelican has the longest wingspan of any bird in Oregon. It flies with its orange bill and long neck tucked back. During the breeding season, the pelican's head becomes slightly black, and a horn grows on the upper mandible. It uses the horn for aggressive behavior during the breeding season. However, it sheds this horn when the breeding season ends. It is present in the Willamette River area, fishing for the river's fish (Fig. 73).

The California brown pelican is one of only two pelican species that feeds by diving into

fig. 72   AMERICAN PEREGRINE FALCON

fig. 73   AMERICAN WHITE PELICAN

the water. It is the smallest species of pelican. It ranges from 42 to 54 inches in length and weighs from 6.1 to 12.1 pounds. Its wingspan ranges from 6.0 to 8.2 feet. The brown pelican has a very large bill with a throat pouch on the bottom for draining water when it scoops out prey. The head is white but often gets a yellowish wash in adult birds. Usually its bill is grayish but can become reddish in breeding birds. Its body is usually gray and dark brown. The legs and feet are black. They are common spring, summer, and fall visitors along the Oregon coast and especially along the Willamette River (Fig. 74).

fig. 74   CALIFORNIA BROWN PELICAN

The American bald eagle feeds mainly on fish, which it snatches from the water of the river with its talons. It is classified as a sea eagle. It builds the largest nest of any North American bird. Bald eagles are not actually bald but instead have white plumage on their head. The adult is mainly brown with a white head and tail and has a large, hooked beak. Females are about 25% larger than males. The bald eagle is both the national bird and national animal of the United States of America. The bald eagle breeds in 32 of 36

fig. 75   BALD EAGLE

Oregon counties and is found throughout the state during nonbreeding season (Fig. 75).

The osprey, also known as the fish eagle, sea hawk, river hawk, and fish hawk, is a large raptor, reaching more than 24 inches in length and 71 inches across the wings. It is brown on the upperparts of its body and mostly grayish on the head and underparts of its body. Its food source is almost entirely fish.

The osprey's weight ranges from 2.0 to 4.6 pounds, and its length ranges from 20 to 26 inches with a 50- to 71-inch wingspan. The osprey is the second most widely distributed raptor species, after the peregrine falcon. In Oregon, ospreys breed statewide except in arid treeless regions of the southeast part of the state. This bird is often seen perched on the river's bridges (Fig. 76).

fig. 76

OSPREY

The double-crested cormorant is the most abundant and widespread of the three cormorant species found in Oregon and on the Willamette River. Adults have black-bordered, coopery feathers that shine with green iridescence. They have a rich orange throat and curved neck. The cormorant has feathers that crown either side of its head during the breeding season. This is how the bird gets its name. They commonly breed in spring and summer in estuaries and bays along the coast of the Willamette River (Fig. 77).

fig. 77   DOUBLE CRESTED CORMORANT

The red-tailed hawk typically weighs from 1.5 to 3.5 pounds and measures 18 to 26 inches in length, with a wingspan from 43 to 57 inches. Generally, this species of hawk is blocky and broad in shape. It has a whitish underbelly with a dark brown band across the belly, formed by horizontal streaks. The species has a red tail, and that is how it gets its name. The tail is uniformly brick red above and light orange below. The hawk's beak is short and hooked. The beak, the legs, and the feet of the red-tailed hawk are all yellow. It is found throughout Oregon in every habitat and at every elevation (Fig. 78).

fig. 78   RED TAILED HAWK

The great blue heron is the largest North American heron. It has a length of 36 to 54 inches, a wingspan of 166 to 79 inches, and a height of 45 to 54 inches. It weighs between 4.0 and 7.9 pounds. It has gray flight feathers with a slight azure blue, red-brown thighs, and a paired red-brown and black stripe up the flanks. The neck is gray, with black and white streaking down the front. The head is paler, and the face is nearly white. A pair of black or slate plumes runs from just above the eye to the back of the head. The bill is dull yellowish, becoming orange briefly at the start of the breeding season, and the lower legs are gray, also becoming orangey at the start of the breeding season. The great blue heron is found commonly throughout Oregon and particularly in the Willamette River area (Fig. 79).

fig. 79

GREAT BLUE HERON

The **Townsend's big-eared bat** is a medium-sized bat with extremely long, flexible ears, and small yet noticeable lumps on each side of the snout. Its total length is around 4 inches, and its wingspan is about 11 inches. The bat requires large cavities for roosting. These may include abandoned buildings and mines, caves, and basal cavities of trees. This species feeds primarily on moths. The Townsend's big-eared bat is really sensitive to human disturbance. Recently, their numbers have been declining, but they sometimes can be seen in the evening from Tilikum Crossing. In Oregon, it is classified as a sensitive species. It is found throughout most of Oregon (Fig. 80).

TOWNSEND BIG EARED BAT

fig. 80

The **California sea lion** has a slender and tapering body. The flippers are relatively small, and like all otariids, the rear flippers can be rotated beneath the body for moving about on land. It does not have a dense under fur, and when dry, its fur is usually chocolate brown. The fur appears black when wet. The occurrence of the California sea lion along the Oregon coast is seasonal. Many enter rivers to feed, including the Willamette. The sea lion is

CALIFORNIA SEA LION

fig. 81

103

a predator for the fish in the river and usually stays around the piers of the bridges (Fig. 81).

Steelhead trout can reach up to 55 pounds and 45 inches. However, the average is much smaller. They are mostly dark olive green with silver-white shading on their underside. They are speckled with a pink stripe running along the side of the body. Uniquely, individuals of this species develop differently according to their environment. While all steelhead trout hatch in fast-flowing, well-oxygenated rivers and streams, some stay in fresh water all their lives, and some migrate to the ocean. The freshwater trout are known as rainbow trout. The ocean-migrating steelheads are slimmer with more silver and typically grow much larger than rainbow trout. Rainbow trout are commonly found in the Willamette River (Fig. 82).

Chinook salmon, also known as the tyee or king salmon, is the largest species of salmon in the Pacific Ocean. It averages 22 pounds, and its body is silvery with a bluish back. As the spawning season approaches, the salmon gets darker in color. The salmon mature in their third to eighth season of life. They return to the freshwater streams they were born in to spawn and then die. They are identified by the time of year they enter fresh water on their spawning migration: spring, summer, or fall.

Salmon were a major food source for the coastal Native American communities. Because of this, the tribes held them in high regard. Many legends, special rites, and taboos were connected with the coming of salmon (Fig. 83).

fig. 82   STEELHEAD TROUT

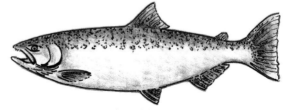

fig. 83   CHINOOK SALMON

Green sturgeons are native to the Pacific Ocean and are found off the coast of Oregon and in the Willamette River. Sturgeons are highly adapted for preying on bottom-dwelling animals, which they detect with a row of sensitive barbells on the underside of their snouts. They are green in color and can reach lengths up to seven feet and weigh up to 350 pounds. Green sturgeon can live as long as 70 years (Fig. 84).

Cutthroat trout coloration can range from golden to gray to green on the back. The name "cutthroat" comes from the distinctive red coloration on the underside of the lower jaw. Cutthroats do not confine themselves strictly to salt water or fresh water. Many may run in and out of streams in search of food. At maturity they go to the rivers, including the Willamette, to spawn (Fig. 85).

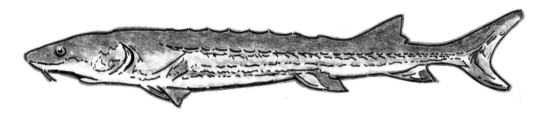

fig. 84 GREEN STURGEON

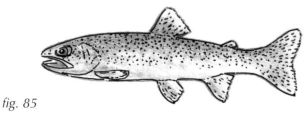

fig. 85

CUTTHROAT TROUT

The Pacific lamprey is a parasitic lamprey that ranges in the Pacific from the coast of Asia to the coast of North America, including the Willamette River. They grow to about 31 inches as adults but spend the majority of their life in the larvae stage. They have slender, long bodies with two fins near the end of their body. Adults living in the sea are a bluish-black or greenish color above and pale below, but those in fresh water are brown (Fig. 86).

fig. 86   PACIFIC LAMPREY

The western painted turtle grows up to 10 inches long. The turtle's top shell is dark and smooth, without a ridge. Its skin is olive to black with red, orange, or yellow stripes on its extremities. The western painted turtle has a red pattern on its bottom shell, and its top shell has a netlike pattern of lines. Its bottom shell has a large colored spot that spreads to the edges and often has red hues. In Oregon, its range includes the lower Willamette Valley. It is listed as critical on Oregon's sensitive species list (Fig. 87).

fig. 87   WESTERN PAINTED TURTLE

Winner of the American Segmental Bridge Institute's 2015 Bridge Award of Excellence, Tilikum Crossing has also received the 2015 Excellence in Concrete award from the Oregon Concrete & Aggregate Producers Association, as well as the People's Choice Award for 2016 from the American Council of Engineering Companies of Oregon.

Additionally, The America Council of Engineering Companies of Oregon named it project of the year for 2016. Additional awards include the Gold Award, Structural Systems, 2016, American Council of Engineering Companies.

Other features: Figures 88 & 89.

TRIMET'S ORANGE LINE LOGO · 2015

fig. 88

TRIMET'S LIGHT RAIL TRAM · 2015

fig. 89

APPENDIX

The People of the Portland Bridges

Goodyear, David. Project Engineer for T.Y. Lin.

Lindenthal, Gustav. Responsible for Ross Island Bridge design, design of Sellwood's truss spans, and construction of Burnside Bridge. Had served as New York City Commissioner of Bridges.

MacDonald, Donald. San Francisco architect, former consulting architect of the Golden Gate responsible for new toll booths, seismic upgrade, bike rail. Designer of the award-winning Cooper River Bridge of Charleston, South Carolina, and of the new Bay Bridge connecting Oakland with Yerba Buena Island. Designer of the new Tilikum Crossing bridge, Portland, Oregon.

Modjeski, Ralph. Designed Broadway Bridge and what is now called the BNSF railroad spans. Designed B. Franklin Bridge (Philadelphia-Camden bridge), at the time the longest suspension span in the world when opened in 1926.

Parsons, Brinckerhoff, Quade & Douglas of New York City. Designed Fremont Bridge.

Steinman, David. Expert on aerodynamics; designed, worked on the St. Johns Bridge.

Strauss, Joseph. Chief Engineer of the Golden Gate Bridge. Held the patent for the Burnside Bridge lift.

Swigert, Charles F. Head of Pacific Bridge Company, oversaw construction of Portland's first Willamette River bridge, the Morrison Street Bridge.

Treyger, Semyon. Engineer and project manager for Tilikum Crossing from inception to completion working for HNTB Corporation.

Waddell & Harrington. Designed the Steel and Hawthorne Bridges.

PARTICIPANTS OF THE TILIKUM CROSSING BRIDGE PROCESS AND FINAL DESIGN

Project Team

Prime Contractor: Kiewit Infrastructure West Co.

Architect: MacDonald Architects

Conceptual Engineering Design: HNTB Corporation

Bridge Engineer for Contractor: T.Y. Lin International

Lighting and Acoustic Discs: Anna Valentina Murch, Douglas Hollis, Morgan Barnard

Portland-Milwaukie Light Rail Transit Steering Committee

Neil McFarlane, General Manager, TriMet

Dan Blocher, Executive Director of Capital Projects, TriMet

Jim Bernard, Commissioner, Clackamas County

Mark Gamba, Mayor, City of Milwaukie

Carlotta Collette, Councilor, Metro

Deborah Kafoury, Commissioner, Multnomah County

Dan Holladay, Mayor, Oregon City

Rian Windsheimer, Region 1 Manager, Oregon Department of Transportation

Patrick Quinton, Executive Director, Portland Development Commission

Willamette River Bridge Advisory Committee

Mayor Vera Katz, Chair

Bob Durgan

Thomas Hacker

Art Johnson

Sue Keil

David Knowles

Pat LaCrosse

Guenevere Millius

Karl Rhode

David Soderstrom

Chuck Steinwandel

Mark Williams

Rick Williams

Mike Zillis

TriMet

Neil McFarlane, General Manager

Daniel W. Blocher, PE, Executive Director of Capital Projects

Ann Becklund, Director of Community Affairs

Robert J. Barnard, AIA, Director of Portland-Milwaukie Light Rail Project

David Tertadian, PE, Tilikum Crossing Project Manager

Bob Hastings, FAIA, Agency Architect

Bridge Statistics

Length: 1,720 feet

Rise: 180 feet pier cap to top

Construction: Concrete, cable-stayed

Completed: 2015

Sources

Bottenberg, Ray. *Bridges of Portland.* Charleston, SC: Arcadia Publishing, 2007.

Boyd, Robert T., Kenneth M. Ames, and Tony A. Johnson, eds. *Chinookan Peoples of the Lower Columbia.* Seattle, WA: University of Washington Press, 2013.

Jespen, Sue. "The Really Big One and Portland." *Oregonian*, July 15, 2015. http://www.oregonlive.com/earthquakes/index.ssf/2015/07/the_really_big_one_and_portlan.html.

Newcomb, Tim. "Portland is Set to Open a Beautiful $135 Million Bridge You Can't Drive Across," *Popular Mechanics*, August 20, 2015. Illustrated.

http://www.popularmechanics.com/technology/infrastructure/g2136/portland-tillikum-crossing-bridge-no-cars/.

Paguio, Clifford. "Tilikum Bridge Aerial Video of Pedestrian Opening." YouTube, August 9, 2015. https://www.youtube.com/watch?v=xxTHL2iUx-U. Excellent view from the air via a drone.

Schulz, Kathryn. "The Really Big One." *New Yorker*, July 20, 2015. Earthquakes in the Northwest.

Treyger, Semyon, and David Tertadian. "The People's Bridge." *Civil Engineering*, April 2016, 53–59.

TriMet. "Tilikum Crossing." http://trimet.org/tilikum. Outstanding site on the history, design, and function of the bridge.

Wortman, Sharon Wood and Ed Wortman. *The Portland Bridge Book*. 3rd Edition. Ed. Ed Wortman and Charlie White. Photographs by James Norman. Portland, OR: Urban Adventures Press, 2006.

INDEX

Donald MacDonald is an international award-winning architect and the designer of the Tilikum Crossing Bridge. He also designed the east span of the San Francisco Oakland Bay Bridge, and was the first architect to work on the Golden Gate Bridge since its original construction. He lives in San Francisco.

Ira Nadel, Professor of English at University of British Columbia, is a Fellow of the Royal Society of Canada and the recipient of numerous awards and prizes. He has lectured around the world and is the author of a number of books, including biographies of Leonard Cohen, Tom Stoppard, Ezra Pound, David Mamet, and Virginia Woolf. He lives in Vancouver, BC.

Donald MacDonald and Ira Nadel have previously co-authored three books together: *Golden Gate Bridge: History and Design of an Icon*, *Bay Bridge: History and Design of a New Icon*, and *Alcatraz: History and Design of a Landmark*.